MW00328002

DOING TIME

DOING TIME

Finding
Hope at
San Quentin

DENNIS BURKE

Paulist Press
New York/Mahwah, NJ

The scripture quotations contained herein come from various versions. These quotations occurred during conversations as recollected by the author and may differ in language or continuity from the actual quotation. However, the language used when people quoted particular passages is often directly related to the circumstances, so no versions have been cited, nor corrections made.

Cover design by Sharyn Banks
Book design by Lynn Else

Library of Congress Cataloging-in-Publication Data

Burke, Dennis.
    Doing time : finding hope at San Quentin / Dennis Burke.
        p. cm.
    ISBN-13: 978-0-8091-4527-0 (alk. paper)
    1. Church work with prisoners—California. 2. Burke, Dennis. I. Title.
    BV4340.B86 2008
    259′.50979462—dc22

                                                            2007048003

Published by Paulist Press
997 Macarthur Boulevard
Mahwah, New Jersey 07430

www.paulistpress.com

Printed and bound in the
United States of America

For Patty, Paul, Peter, Amy, and Baby Jesse

CONTENTS

ACKNOWLEDGMENTS

A debt of gratitude to Father Dennis McManus, without whom I would never have ventured into San Quentin prison; to Father Jack O'Neill, dear friend and for twenty years the legendary chaplain there; to Father Stephen Barber, SJ, current chaplain; and to all the great people that I have come to know in prison ministry at the Q, especially George Salenger, Fred Juul, John, Roberto, Marx Casenave, Sister Karen, Lisa Fullam, Deacon Ed Cunningham, Deacon Bernie O'Halloran, and his wife Dolores.

I am grateful to all the men I have met at the Q: the "gang of ten"; my Patten College students and those in the RCIA; the men from the Protestant chapel at the Christmas party; and the countless, nameless men I met walking the tiers and through the vast prison yard. They all have a part of my heart.

Also, many thanks to Father Mike Kerrigan, CSP, and Father Larry Boadt, CSP, for their invaluable suggestions and support in the process of getting *Doing Time* into print.

In the prisoners' best interests, I have changed all their names in the book.

1

HOOKED BY THE Q

Prison is a grim, forbidding place where two men are crammed into a one-man cell not much bigger than a narrow closet and deprived of their freedom, dignity, and self-respect. It's a place where people—other than inmates—don't return your smile or hello easily unless they've seen your face for a long time and you're considered part of the team. It's a place where words like *monotonous, depressing,* and *hopeless* are reflected in a lifer's eyes. It's a place that's been willfully forgotten. Entering through the gates is like entering a walled kingdom under a wicked spell where time stands still for five-thousand men. Yet, for outsiders, there is a certain fascination and attraction about a prison. And sometimes curiosity leads to commitment.

I got involved at San Quentin almost accidentally. The year was 1996. Father Dennis McManus, the prison chaplain, was in residence at my local parish and asked if I would like to help out at the prison on Sundays. He's a cautious recruiter—"prison ministry isn't for everyone"—but he had been eyeing my dormant priesthood for some time. Looking at me and shaking his head, he said to me once, "What a waste." I agreed to sign up for a "brown card." From then on, the experience was so intense I feel like I am still living out each day right now…

—⁂—

There are eighty people at the first brown-card sign-up meeting. Some look like they have been through the wars: group leaders from AA and NA (Narcotics Anonymous), or from anger management classes. Their chiseled bodies and scarred black faces say they were probably inside the Q at one time themselves. But most are connected in one way or another with a church or a temple or some place of education. An old Black man—dressed primly in a starched collar, tie, and cheap herringbone sport coat, his black hair whitening about the temples and mustache—introduces himself to me as "an apostle of the Lord Jesus Christ to preach the gospel." Rastafarians, Muslims, Native Americans, Christians, Pentecostals, and a cluster of educators who teach in the GED or two-year college program: this is the mix that shows up at the meeting. There are the young idealists, but most of the volunteers are from Berkeley across the bay and are older. They have the time. There are other brown-card meetings, and the total number of volunteers is in the hundreds—probably the largest number of volunteers at any prison in the United States. Not surprisingly, San Quentin has a history of using outside resources to humanize and rehabilitate the inmates. Not a penny comes from the state because the politicians want to appear tough on crime. But San Quentin's Jeanie Woodford is good about allowing and even supporting free help.

At this, my first brown-card meeting, the prison's director of community resources leads us through those parts of the state criminal code that concern volunteers: how we should dress—"nothing blue" (the color worn by most of the prisoners); what we can give—"nothing"; what we should do if accosted by a prisoner—"blow your whistle." Numerous past mistakes by volunteers are cited, along with the negative consequence: "loss of brown card." We are then shown a training film for prison guards that emphasizes the "con" in convict: how a con works hard to make friends with a guard, to get him or her to compromise themselves by breaking the rule. Once a guard is compromised by passing a note, slipping a con a couple of cigarettes, or making a phone call, the con has power over the guard and can blackmail him to smuggle drugs. Every so often, a bulky prison psychiatrist from Georgia or Alabama, with a stern look and ominous tone, appears on the video to reinforce the intrinsic duplicity of all convicts. "*Never, never* believe a con! You cannot trust them." While there is no small amount of conning and deception by the inmates, and while many are virtually incorrigible, it is not quite as bleak as the psychiatrist on the video says. But he makes a point.

One of the first Sundays I come to the prison for my monthly communion service, in which I distribute already-consecrated hosts, I am greeted by Roberto, a gentle man from San Francisco. He is the maître d' and concierge in one, answering questions and greeting the mainline choir members and chapel clerks in English or Spanish; "mainline" prisoners are those in the general population, neither newly incarcerated, nor in maximum security. For fifteen years Roberto has been at the Q every Sunday. He visits the men in the cellblocks, bringing the Eucharist, pamphlets, and rosaries with him. Two Sisters of Charity, members of Mother Teresa's community, also visit the men. Maybe because they look like doubles for Mother Teresa in their blue-trimmed saris, the tough, gruff guards are melted by the faces of sweet, simple, sandal-wearing nuns and let them into parts of the prison cellblocks where few are allowed.

After the communion service, Roberto takes me along as he visits some prisoners in Alpine, one of the four sections of South Block. He tries to enlist me to join him on Sundays but

I demur, saying, "The 49ers play on Sunday." Roberto smiles sadly.

At the time, six hours preparing a homily, three hours waiting for the guards to release the men for chapel, and an hour or so running the service seem enough for me to feel virtuous without heavy involvement. Besides, I have a busy life being president of a small international consulting firm and writing suspense novels on airplanes in the cracks of time. I am not a well-known author because I specialize in unpublished novels. But like the prisoners, I have hopes. It never enters my head to write a book about the Q.

In a priest-friendly way, if not deeply, I get to know the mainliners in blue denim who "run" the chapel. These mainliners are atypical of the majority of prisoners at the Q so I have to keep reminding myself they did something bad once, maybe twice. Steve of the red hair, easy smile, and sweet guitar leads the choir. I tell him one Sunday his beautiful music is better than the music in my parish. He answers dryly: "We have more time to practice." Big-chested, low-voiced Phil is the head honcho in the sacristy, worrying about supplies and leaks in the roof. Oscar, the only Black in the choir, bangs on the drums and blesses the Lord. These and a dozen others have become, in prison parlance, "spiritual." And the men in the orange jumpsuits who rotate in and out of the Q I don't know at all except to shake their hands and say "Peace of Christ" during the liturgy.

So, for four years, I bop in and out like this, one Sunday a month. Then my partner buys me out of the business, and suddenly I find myself with more time. I get an itch to visit the men in the cellblocks. What is the draw: Curiosity? Compassion for the men in cages? The need to do penance for my own sins? Human decency? After all, I am here and can visit them.

Maybe it's all of these and more, as I age and feel the need, in Jacques Maritain's phrase, "to ransom the time."

I approach Father McManus, the chaplain of Catholic ministry, who recruited me four years ago. He is a shy, complex Irishman who has seen it all: from every serial killer in California the past twenty years to lions devouring wildebeests in Africa as a missionary for ten years. He sits behind his simple government-issued desk in his cramped chapel-vestibule office, walled in by books of every kind, especially theological and biblical. It is his duty to inform a prisoner through the bars—over the din of shouts and bellows and cursing of five-hundred men—that his wife or child or mother has died. Father McManus pretends not to see the tears of the prisoner who is doubly stricken by the death and by his own inability to be present at the last moment: one more reminder of his failed life. It is McManus's duty to be the only human bridge between the cold prison walls and the outside world of family joys and miseries. And also his duty to offer the Mass on Sundays and on death row as Charles Manson, the Hillside Strangler, and others almost as infamous look on without faith or comprehension.

McManus is a handsome, silver-haired Obi-Wan Kenobi with a soft Dublin accent. His mind is quick, his judgment considered, his tongue often sharp. Sometimes his clear blue eyes twinkle with glee, and a deliciously wicked smile breaks his lips as he reveals some "humanoid" has "bollixed it up again." Other times, there is a wariness and a cock of the head that says, "You can't be serious." His sardonic style tickles me.

I tell him I would like to visit the men in the cellblocks. McManus, who has that terrible Irish fear of being a fool, gives me a "reverse sell." "It's not for everyone," he tells me. "You may not like it." I sense he is secretly hoping I will not hear him.

"People come and do it once and never come back again." He thinks some more. "Are you *shure* you want to do it? I'd rather have you for Sundays if anything." And after I start visiting the men in the cellblocks, he says, "Don't visit the cellblocks for more than two hours at a time. You'll burn out." He is not wrong. Prison burnout is common. But secretly he is excited that I am getting more involved. I am hooked by the Q and one of the reasons is McManus.

2
FIRST TIME IN THE CELL BLOCKS

On a cool Monday morning, George Salinger and I walk out of the prison chapel and the quad to the long upper yard with its corrugated tin roof against the rain, and its guard-snipers up above in their catbird seats. Here and there some mainliners in blue, smoking or standing or sitting around lethargically, stare vacantly at us as we pass by. They are on work breaks or are "maintaining" the yard. I am quietly excited at the prospect of doing what few people ever do: mingle with the prisoners, get into their murky pasts, give them some hope.

Deacon George, as Salinger is called, will be my mentor the first time or two through the cellblocks to make sure I don't do anything stupid. A prison, by its very nature, is a quintessential police state. The rules are there for a pretty good reason. Violations—even unconscious ones—can be dangerous to someone's health. Deacon George will also model for me the way he has been doing prison ministry for some years at San Quentin. "Not everyone can do this kind of work, you know.

DOING TIME

You need a spiritual life and some spiritual depth." Deacon George has been to hell and back in his life,—losing his family, job, and home. He had to hit bottom before coming back up. So, he's very spiritual now. He talks like an inmate. The prison has become his life.

We approach South Block, which holds 1,750 prisoners in four sections named after mountain passes: Donner, Alpine, Carson, and Badger. The latter two sections house industrial-strength criminals and only a state-paid chaplain is allowed to go in there. Deacon George and I enter through the heavy steel door of Donner and show our brown cards to the sergeant at the counter. There are usually three or four guards—in olive-green uniforms, black belts, boots, and clubs—at the counter and the narrow hole-in-the-wall office. They have data cards on the prisoners, as the population is constantly changing. Most prisoners are transferred within ninety days. The guards spend a lot of time taking count, herding groups to mess hall, or escorting individuals to medical appointments or visits with their counselors. Counselors do little, if any, counseling. Mostly, they evaluate prisoner backgrounds and histories, decide the best location for each inmate, and select cellmates, called *cellies,* least likely to kill each other.

Donner has five tiers with steel railings and a steel staircase in the middle. There are a hundred men on each tier, two to a cell designed for one. I stretch my neck, look up, and think of a giant five-story birdhouse with bars on the holes. The cells look out to a grimy cream-colored wall and opaque, weather-dirtied windows that give faint light and no view of the outside world. The concrete floors are shiny, smooth, and darkened from shellac and the steps of thousands of prisoners. The railings are smooth where they are not chipped and have been painted over. It's an old prison. The new high-tech supermax prisons sparkle and gleam with fluorescent silence, belying the mental torture of total isolation and abandonment. For all its grimness and lack of gloss, the Q has it all over them, the inmates tell me. It has a certain homey quality about it, as prisons go. It has *soul*.

The first tier has a number of cells with the sign "Single Cell" on them. This usually means that a man is paranoid or psychotic, potentially dangerous to himself and others. We look into the darkness of a cell. Then another. The inmates are asleep at ten in the morning and when they wake, they likely will be distant or subdued. The men on the first tier are heavily medicated—like many others in the prison. If an inmate says he can't take it emotionally, he is prescribed lithium or another drug and he sleeps his time away. Crime and mental illness are no strangers, and since Reagan shut down the mental institutions the line between crime and psychosis is often blurred. After a while I will think at moments that there is a screw loose or a circuit broken or a drive "out of sync" in almost everyone here. But not necessarily. For some it is just a bad day maybe, and maybe just this once.

Deacon George and I make clanking sounds as we ascend the steep steel staircase to the second tier and make our rounds. Our sounds are lost in the din of prisoners' shouts and hollers and bellowing up and down the tiers. Sometimes there is a request for a chaplain sent by a "kite," a written note passed from one inmate to the next till it reaches its goal. Most of the time there is not one for the chaplain most kites are sent from one gang member to another.

We stop at a cell. I observe Deacon George. He is perfect for this job. He looks like Popeye. He has the bulbous nose, the squinty-eyed look, and the puffy-cheeked face. He even has the gravelly voice.

"Parole violation?" Deacon George inquires. He already has the man's CDC (California Department of Corrections) number. The CDC is a giveaway. If it begins with an early letter in the alphabet, it means that this is not the first time. This inmate has an H.

"Yeah," answers a grizzled man in his late forties. He is white, a minority here, his forearms grotesquely tattooed.

"How many times you been in here?"

The prisoner, clinging to the bars, thinks about it, cocking his head to count.

"Seven times."

"You must like it here," Deacon George says with a grim smile. "Drugs and alcohol part of the problem?" It almost always is. A crime is often what lands a man in prison, but it's often drugs that force him to commit the crime, and then, later, drugs that make him a "parole violator."

"Drugs."

"Meth?"

"Coke."

"Been through drug rehab I bet."

"Yeah. Twice. Didn't work."

"You didn't really want to give it up did you?" Another grim, knowing smile from Deacon George.

"I wanted to," the inmate protests, "but it's hard. Tried drug rehab twice but had to drop out. Had to make some money. My girlfriend's got two kids." He pauses. "I'm clean for three months, then the pressure builds and some guy at work...You know...."

"Yeah, I know. You're kidding yourself. I know because I kidded myself for twenty-five years."

"Whaddaya mean?"

"I drank for twenty-five years. Lost my wife, my kids. They wouldn't talk to me the last fifteen. I slept under the Bay Bridge in a cardboard box for a while. My older brother, Pierre, had to drag me out of the Bowery in New York once." This is the same Pierre who was press secretary to JFK and ambassador to France. "I went to AA meetings and faked it. I would tell my story then go across the street to a bar and get drunk. And you know why?"

"Why?"

"Because I felt lousy about myself, that's why."

I can see that register with the con, the last vestige of cockiness slipping off his face. Low self-esteem is usually the heart of the problem.

"But I finally hit bottom," Deacon George says, continuing. "Went through rehab, AA, and been clean and sober for twenty-five years. Thank God."

The grizzled con is trying to absorb all this. There is lots of time to think in prison. The problem is that you're clean and sober or drug-free in prison not by your own willpower but by the will of the state. So, the con often seduces himself into thinking he's licked it or can do so by his own willpower.

"How are you doing spiritually?" Deacon George asks.

"I'm readin' the Bible." Almost every prisoner has a Bible or a New Testament. Prisoners tend to get more spiritual in prison, especially those who are addicted and know it and are desperate.

"Let's pray," Deacon George says.

The three of us join hands through the bars. George prays, "Oh God, how you love us. And your love is unconditional. Help Charlie to believe that no matter what he does you still love him. Help him. Give him courage and strength to kick his addiction. He can't do it without you." Deacon George pauses. "Who'd you like to pray for?"

The con mentions his girlfriend and her kids, his mom and dad, his cellie, even the guards. He tells Deacon George he would like to talk to him again. George promises to return. We move on. There are only five thousand more prisoners to see.

3

TATTOOS, GRILLED CHEESE, AND CLYDE THE GLIDE

Monday, four years after I first set foot in the Q, I begin to visit men in the cellblocks. It is still a novelty, this prison world, and it is hard for me to realize the Q and everyone in it will soon be the staple of my life.

I start at the chapel office by shooting the breeze with McManus and Deacon George. There is often something funny, plain wacko, or terribly sad that has happened since the previous week: a rumored prison break or a brawl that leads to restricted movement for all Latinos, say, or a suicide. Suicides are handled discreetly by guards in the early morning hours. "All you hear is the patter of feet," one prisoner tells me. For reasons of morale, the prisoners assume. I pump McManus for weird cases. He sits back, squeezes his chin, and reflects. "There was the guy who cut off his tongue because it had caused him so much trouble. *If your hand scandalizes you cut it off.* And another guy, in a fit of biblical passion, tried to circumcise himself and almost bled to death in his cell." McManus shakes his head. "It just shows that literal interpretation of the Bible can be dangerous to your health." We sprinkle the serious talk with gallows or lethal-injection humor and get ready for the morning.

11

I stuff my pockets with *Daily Bread*s (daily meditations on the scripture that come out quarterly), with centering-prayer pamphlets from the Trappists, with a requested New Testament, and with small plastic packets of cheap rosaries with instructions in Spanish and English. "Don't give them to guys who are going to wear them around their necks," McManus hollers from his office. But sometimes I forget and and a half dozen guys, usually Blacks, have them around their necks like pious nooses. McManus is appalled by superstition: Baptists wearing rosaries as a talisman, a good luck piece. But "faith is closer to superstition than reason," John Henry Newman once said. And as long as they don't strangle their cellie with it—you never know. Now we pass out smaller rosaries that won't fit over the neck. I always tell them, "You're supposed to *pray* the Rosary." *"Pray it?"* some answer with surprise and disappointment. But we pass out an instructional booklet with each rosary and some who are not Catholic actually pray it—meditating on the mysteries of Christ's life as they say Hail Marys.

George and I stride across the courtyard outside the chapel, past "the adjustment center" (mother of all euphemisms), better known as "the hole," solitary confinement. We also pass the 4-post, the central control point between North, South, East, and West Blocks. It reminds me that the Q is an antique prison, which accounts for much of its "charm." Nothing cold or high tech about it. The 4-post is a quaint turn-of-the-century structure, a ten-sided, glassed-in gazebo. It houses an officer, under the watch commander, with a vast assortment of keys.

As we pass the ancient administration and education building on our right, George gives me more last-minute instructions in his deep, whiskey-burned, master-sergeant voice: "I always wash my hands after time in the cellblocks, especially before lunch. You never know." He gives me a look that says *A word to the wise.* I almost smile because George was half-pickled a good part of his life, sleeping under the Bay Bridge in a cardboard box or a gutter in the New York Bowery, and I figure if that didn't kill him, nothing will. But George is absolutely right. I will touch or shake a hundred hands this morning through the bars and black steel grating, or in the vast yard or the long walk to the cellblocks. And prisoners are rife with TB, VD, HIV/AIDS, and nasal-dripping colds and hacking coughs in the fall and winter. The fresh phlegmy spittings that I sidestep on the asphalt remind me of that as we near the cellblocks. *I will wash my hands, George, just like you do.*

And so my street education begins. As George moves on to Carson and Badger cellblocks where the harder cases are, I grunt to pull open the ancient steel door to Donner. A couple of guards are clustered around a wooden stand outside a tiny office. The narrow office, the size of a cell, has a wall with five-hundred "time card" slots for the five-hundred guys doing time. The constant shuffling of prisoners from one cellblock to another, or one prison to another, makes record-keeping and count-taking a never-ending task. I sign in the brown-card logbook to a collection of cool, impersonal looks. They don't know me yet. I'm a new player in the system. It will take a few years before they see me as part of the aged concrete and rusty steel like them.

I walk past two large stand-alone cages on my left. A cage with a human being in it reminds me of the starkness of their condition, even though the caged are probably just waiting to see the doctor or their counselor, or to be transferred. I pound up the metal stairs to the second tier. A big Black guy gets my attention.

"Counselor!" he shouts, his head pressed into the bars he grips tightly.

"Catholic ministry," I respond.

"You a priest?" Blacks respect a priest, even though 95 percent of them are Baptist. They see him as a man of God.

"Kind of," I say. After a while I will sometimes answer yes because that's what they intuitively think I am and it happens to be true. I lean against the bars to better see this big dark man in his tiny dark cell. "So, how's it going?"

"I was doin' *fine*. Comin' along real good except for that *one woman*." He's got a deep, husky voice and is heavy set. His kinky hair is graying around the temples.

"Drugs?"

"*No*. It was just that *one woman*."

"She was doing drugs?" I have a hunch.

"Yeah." He sighs disgustedly. *"That one woman."* He's obviously a repeater and repeaters tend to project their problems onto others. But maybe this guy is right. Maybe it was that one woman.

I listen to him for a while, wondering whether I would do drugs if *I* were in his shoes: Poor. Black. In and out of menial, low-paying jobs. Living in a dirt front house in East Oakland. Barely able to read and write. Living in the culture of failure. And I'm not sure. We touch fingers through the black grate, bow our heads, and pray. Black men pray by instinct I will find; without hesitation or embarrassment. And they pray from the heart.

"That *one woman*," he mutters as I leave. Adam said the same thing about Eve.

I climb to the next tier and look down three iron staircases to the concrete below. Donner looks and feels like a tenement and in a way it is: Two men jammed into one-man cells.

DOING TIME

Guys with beery, right-field bleacher-voices hollering back and forth through the bars to their buddies. Others dropping strings with notes or small packets of barter to a tier below. Barter is money, cigarettes, stamps, or a favor. Despite the noise, half the men are doing time asleep under the covers, trying to blank it out. Dogs sleep an average of eighteen hours a day. Cons, since they have nothing to do, match it.

I spot some activity. A white guy, stripped to the waist and tattooed from the neck down, is lighting bits of paper in a Styrofoam cup. At the same time, he is talking to a young con outside his cell who, with his blonde, shaven head, looks like a point guard for the Sacramento Kings. I hear the man in the cell say that the kid can shake his addiction to crack if he joins NA (Narcotics Anonymous). The kid doubts it. "I like the stuff," he says. The wise man in the cell, who I find is a tattoo artist, responds with cheery cynicism: "You need faith in a higher power. But the higher power can be your wife, your dog, your car—anything greater than you." All the while, the tattoo artist is mincing a hot chili for a cheese sandwich he is grilling over the smoking Styrofoam cup.

You may wonder how a man can tattoo in prison. Prisoners are ingenious at making do: First, you barter with a buddy to swipe a couple of used hypodermic needles from the infirmary. If he can't, then a paper clip, a guitar string, or perhaps a pen will do. Then you barter and sweet-talk until you get a guard to bring in the "juice"—meaning the ink—for the needle. Easy as pie they tell me. How else do the prisoners make do? Handguns out of cardboard hardened over a Styrofoam cup fire. Shivs, or knives, out of metal bed parts, ripped off by brute force then ingeniously, patiently sharpened to a fine, deadly edge.

I leave. A few minutes later, I run into the kid with the shaved head again and he proudly shows me the blackened white toast of the grilled-cheese sandwich the tattoo artist has just made for him. I am impressed. It looks "like mother used to make."

In a neighboring cell there are a couple of Black guys. I talk to one for a while. "How you doing? Where you from?" And so forth. He's one more parole violator struggling with demons. I ask about his cellie. His cellie slithers toward me in the darkness between the bed and the wall in the hellishly cramped quarters. His glossy bedroom eyes flash at me out of his well-featured ebony face.

"You don't want to talk to me," he says with a smooth smile.

"Why not?" I ask.

"I'm Clyde the Glide. I'm a pimp. I'm evil." He laughs. He's trying to shock me. I'm not shocked. I've seen most everything in life. If I didn't hear it in the confessional, I observed it when I worked in the studios in Hollywood during high school. But I'm bugged. Most inmates in Donner are regretful and even hang-dog repentant about their addictions or violence or stupidity. But this guy is proud of his sin, proud of corrupting the young ladies in his neighborhood, driving slowly down the streets of East Oakland, a pretty whore by his Clyde-the-Glide side.

I stare hard at him, then move on. I'll be back to see him. Something about him gets under my skin.

My legs are getting tired. It's standing on the concrete for so long. My neck hurts from straining to see through the grated, barred darkness of the cells. And the air, after three hours in this 5-tiered bunker of five-hundred men, breathes like a hot, dusty closet.

But then I run into Kevin, a good-looking white guy who made $100,000 a year when his wife left him. The $30,000-a-year alimony sent him into a downward spiral of drinking and drugging. "Then I got into a rehab program and it changed my whole way of thinking. I'm out of here in nine months. I won't be back again."

"Where you at spiritually?" I inquire, leaning against the cell.

"I read the Bible."

Everyone reads the Bible—in prison.

"I used to be Catholic," he blurts. "I went to a priest for help and he let me down."

"There's a lot of good priests. If one doesn't help you, go to another one."

He shrugs bitterly.

"*I* used to be a priest," I say.

He seems to identify with that: somebody else who's human, who failed somehow. We talk for a while. A guard's voice blares over the loudspeaker and guys in orange jumpsuits shuttle past us on the tier.

"Would you like to go to communion?"

"Sure," he says. His face turns serious.

I ask him if he's sorry for his sins. He is. I take the sacred host out of the small gold pyx, tarnished from overuse, and say: "Behold the Lamb of God, behold him who takes away the sins of the world. Lord, I am not worthy that you should come under my roof but say the word and I shall be healed." I hand him the host through a slender opening at the top of the bars. "Body of Christ." He takes it in his fingers, lowers his head. In the banging, restless din, I help him with his thanksgiving. When he looks up at last, he has a different face than when we first started talking. The anger has left it.

As I tromp down the steel steps of the third tier, two Latinos catch my eye. They don't speak much English, and my Spanish will not win any prizes. I have a fairly good accent and

17

enough introductory phrases to get me into trouble. Both José and Miguel are quiet and subdued, descended, probably, from a long line of oppressed peasants.

"*Catolico?*" I ask, to put them at ease.

"*Si,*" one answers. The other nods agreement.

In my fractured Spanish I find out one is from San Jose, California, and the other from Michoacán, Mexico. The one from Michoacán is worried because he will probably be deported to Mexico.

"*Quisiera estar aqui?*" You would rather stay here?

"*Si. No hay cucarachas aqui.*" Yes, there are no cockroaches here.

Everyone has a reason for preferring the Q. For this one it's the absence of cockroaches.

4
CONFRONTING CLYDE THE GLIDE

The next week I get back to the pimp. He's been in my craw all that time. I have a need to wipe the evil smile off his face. My son Paul teaches at Sacred Heart, a Black inner-city school in San Francisco where the kids come out of the projects and only 5 percent are Catholic. One day my son asked me to talk to his kids about writing. I read them a chapter from one of my unpublished novels and said they must have plenty of interesting experiences themselves for stories. I asked each of them to write one down. They giggled, scratched their heads, wrote, and then took turns reading their stories to the class. All but two were about a killing, a shooting, or a robbery of a local store that we could almost see out the classroom window. They shared all this with a mixture of excitement, uneasiness, and fear.

With Clyde the Glide stuck in my head, I remember that the eighth-grade girls—with their big easy smiles, cornrows, and pretty young faces—were unusually tall and well-developed. Scary.

I make my way down the third tier of Donner to the pimp's cell. "I won't even talk to that guy," Deacon George told me on the way this morning.

"I'm gettin' out in a week." Smooth, gloating tones. The pimp anticipated my arrival with a makeshift mirror slipped between the bars.

"What are you going to do when you get out?" I know the answer. Still I ask, then stare at him through the bars.

"I'm gonna pimp." He breaks into a sleazy smile. "That's the life, man. Don't look at me hard like that. I treat my girls well. Tender love, good money, no diseases. *Clean.*"

I stare at him coldly. He grins. Then I tear into him.

"My son teaches in a Black ghetto school. Most of the kids have no future. They don't have a chance in hell of getting out. It's only a matter of time before they go down with crack or a bullet. And you know why? Because young Black girls have been used and abused by guys like you. Half the kids in my son's school have no real mother to speak of because she was turned into a whore by guys like you. That's why poor Black kids don't have a chance."

By the time I finish, the pimp's cockiness is gone. I might be a white person, but my kid is putting his body on the line in the ghetto and the pimp knows it. I move on, surprised I have him thinking about it even a little. It won't last is my guess. The pimp will be swallowed up by his proclivities—what makes a man a pimp?—and the culture of poverty he will soon reenter. Swallowed up as if by a black hole. When I cool down, my heart goes out to him, and I am not proud about losing my temper. Would Christ or Mother Teresa or Gandhi do that? Love, not anger, conquers all in the long run. But a little anger does feel good in the short. Call it tough love.

An hour later I'm in Alpine, the sister cellblock to Donner. Unless there's a lockdown—men confined to their cells for days and without yard breaks—Alpine has their two-hour weekly exercise-break in the yard on Monday mornings about this time. The guard behind the desk is a good guy. His dry sense of humor with the inmates dispels any tension in the block. He is white with slick auburn hair and a laid-back, philosophical attitude. He's seen some of these men sent to the Q a dozen times and knows they'll be back again. I mention last night's TV special on Alexander the Great. The guard says he has read a couple of biographies on Alexander. I'm surprised. *A literate guard.* He must see the look on my face and adds, "I'm a history buff." It's something you wouldn't expect, but guards—like prisoners—are not always what they appear to be.

A white guy in blue denim comes up to me as I sign in at the desk. He is one of the "clerks" assisting the guards and he has that earnest, boyish look of a movie character who might be underhanded.

"I heard you talking last week," he says, and "I'd like to become a Catholic."

"Why?" Usually someone says something like this in a quiet place and only after some serious preliminary confession.

"I have this urge, this drive, to become a Catholic. More than anything."

"What got you interested in—?"

"My mother was a Catholic but was excommunicated for marrying a Mormon, and I'd like to become a priest. Can a guy with my background become a priest?"

"It's possible. A number of excons have made it." But I'm thinking: longest shot of the day.

I promise to bring some books but I'm not quite sure what to make of this guy. He is obviously better educated than the average prisoner, and since he is a clerk for Alpine, I assume he is above-average in virtue and integrity. (I later observe that the guards select clerks on the basis of smarts only.) So, for the moment, I'm excited by the prospect of not just a convert but a future priest. So I fail to read his face with a hard eye. A hint of a smile is ever-lurking on his lips, and he has an awfully easy way with words.

An hour more and I have met, listened to, kidded, exhorted ("hang in there"), or prayed with a half-dozen more men—most of them repeats, not totally unhappy with the opportunity to dry out or get clean or get their act together. One is a handsome Black who played cornerback for the San Diego Chargers until recently, but most men come from less-glamorous pasts and presents: Those on SSI (State Supplementary Income) because of some physical or mental disability who tend to self-medicate. Unskilled workers in construction, warehousing, landscaping, and so on. More than a few skilled carpenters or welders. Even men who own their own contracting business. And, of course, house painters drying out like a fresh coat on a front porch. Is it the paint thinner that does it or the mindlessness of the tasks? But there seems to be a preponderance of house painters.

A tier down I run into a prisoner who tells me this is his fifth time in the slammer. He is not a big man, nor is he muscular like so many others. He has fine curly hair and either a straggly beard or an unshaven face—it's hard to tell. But he looks a little desperate because he *has tried,* he tells me. Eleven months without drugs.

"Meth?"

"Yeah."

But he slipped once after his mother died and his parole officer sent him back. They gave him twelve months. He begged to get into Delancey Street, which is a tough, *tough* rehab program, tougher than the toughest seminary, but he was denied.

He becomes more desperate as he talks and is almost on the verge of tears. He doesn't strike me as a laid-back, good-time, enjoy-the-high kind of guy, but a marked man relentlessly pursued by a killer addiction. He may have been an eager participant in the beginning but he seems all victim now, skidding close to the bottom—if he hasn't reached it already.

I ask him, "You want to give it up more than anything in this world?"

"Yes," he whispers.

"Well, if you *really* want to give it up more than anything in this world, then you've got to follow the disciplines. They're all linked together. You've got to do them all."

I lay out the disciplines, steps as I see them in my short time at the Q. He listens intently. Any straw to grab.

"You have to go through a serious rehab program like Delancey Street or Walden House.

"You have to join AA or NA.

"You have to hook up with a sponsor in NA.

"And you have to find new buddies."

I pause to let it sink in. I see he's nodding his head.

"If you keep running with dogs what do you do?" I ask. He doesn't know. I answer my rhetorical question with a cruder way of saying that he'll start defecating on the lawn. "Saint Paul quotes a pagan author, Menander, to make the same point: *The noblest of people are ruined by bad companions.*"

"My wife does drugs," he says quietly.

I go silent. The enemy is from within. The enemy is his beloved, and he might need heart surgery. The thought of it saddens me. I was going to give him the final discipline—you have to join a faith community that will support you and you have to develop a real relationship with God or…I don't say the words. Maybe after he's figured out the last one about bad companions.

In the face of addiction, I sometimes feel that I'm just throwing words at it, that I'm trying to stop a roaring lion with paper wads.

My legs are weary from standing on the unforgiving concrete floors. But I hardly notice them as I walk past lunch-break mainliners and a restless drove of orange jumpsuits. I'm thinking: *You're in state prison, guys—this is no overnight county-jail lark.* But to some, it seems *prison* is just another word for "drying out."

Back in the chapel I find McManus, Obi-Wan Kenobi, sitting back in his chair, eating a banana, a sardonic smile temporarily missing from his face. McManus and I are roughly the same age but I instinctively see him as wiser than myself. Is it the white goatee or the reserved manner? Anyway, I tell him about the Catholic-Mormon guy who wants to become a Catholic and a *priest* even. I relate the story matter-of-factly, trying to moderate my enthusiasm so as not to appear naive.

That Sunday I tell the grizzled, painted, head-shaved, half-awake inmates in orange jumpsuits—some of whom are there just for a cell break and are twitching, scratching, and grinning with irreverence—about an unforgettable Iranian film I saw recently: *The Color of Paradise.* It opens with Mohammed, an eight-year-old blind boy, waiting for his father outside his special school. He hears the frantic squawking of a tiny bird. He finds the tiny, featherless newborn in the leaves; then, struggling, he climbs the tree, following the mother's peeping sound, and replaces the tiny bird in its nest. The boy sees the beauty of the universe with his fingers: a flower, a butterfly, the wind, a stream, his grandmother's lined face. At the special Muslim school for the blind, he learns: "God is not visible. But you can see him through your fingertips." So, with his finger-tips, he sees God everywhere.

The boy's father, a peasant farmer, recently widowed, feels overwhelmed by his three kids, an aging mother, and long, hard days in the field. He feels burdened, even cursed, by the disabled boy. Who will marry a man with a blind child? He rages against God. Shockingly, he lets the boy wander into the deep woods, pretending not to notice, but a worker does and goes after the boy. Again and again the father, though he has eyes, sees nothing.

Finally, Mohammed, the blind boy, falls into a raging torrent of water while crossing a rickety bridge. The father hesitates for a moment and finally jumps into the white water to save him. The father almost drowns. He finds his son dead on the beach, his fingers up to the sky—bright and expressive as eyes.

The father has to see his son dead before he can under-stand how blind he himself has been, locked up in himself. He has to hit bottom to find he is closed to God's love and to the meaning of life all around him. Isn't this like us? Don't we have to hit bottom before we see the way things really are?

I tell them to ask God for Mohammed's fingertips.

The inmates seem very quiet at the end. Maybe the word has struck home to one person. God knows. That's all I am trying to reach—one person. Catch him off guard. Get him off drugs.

5

A "DIRTY TEST" AND THE PRODIGAL SON

There's less light in a two-man cell than in a mine shaft. There's so little room to stand or sit, the men snooze or read lying down in their bunks. Some stand, holding onto the bars and staring out at the dirty cream walls, and futilely holler, "Counselor! Hey counselor!"

Counselors don't counsel. They make decisions on when and where an inmate is going next in the system: the mainline at the Q or another prison altogether. In the mainline a man junks his orange jumpsuit for blue jeans and a light-blue denim shirt and has much more freedom to come and go within the prison: to school, to work, to chapel if on a list for it, and so on. A man is stuck in the "reception" center and not allowed to make a phone call for sixty to ninety days, and even months longer. Sometimes the men don't know for weeks or months the exact charge they face or the length of their sentence. An inmate is required to be "processed" within sixty to ninety days—but the shortage of prisons, the volume of prisoners, and the ridiculously long sentences for nonviolent crime help lengthen the stays in the reception center. If the poor had first-rate legal counsel, there would be plenty of room in California prisons. They might be half empty, in fact.

"Counselor!"

"Catholic ministry," I answer if I have no particular destination.

I listen to his story. His girlfriend is pregnant, and she doesn't know where he is. And his great grandmother had a stroke—six months ago. Can I get him a phone call? Either a priest or myself as chaplain can arrange a phone call—if it involves something serious or urgent like a dying parent or other family member. But cons and their families often lie to get a phone call, so McManus and Deacon George and I won't ask the guards unless we or the prisoner can verify it. Most of the time if the corpse is not at the mortuary—no phone call.

I pass an inmate with a twirly red mustache, a wrinkled neck, and the saddest look. I stop, lean into the bars that hold him, and draw out his story. He tells me he lives in a trailer on the farm where he works up north near Yuba City. He goes to Calvary Baptist Church on Sundays pretty regular. Been dry for quite a spell but violated parole with a "dirty test." Sometimes a man makes it sound like he's not really an alcoholic or a druggie—he just doesn't do well on tests. But this man's face is a mea culpa. I ask him, "You know the parable of the prodigal son?" A small light of recognition goes on in his eyes. I tell him the most beautiful parable in the gospels. How this son takes his inheritance from his father and blows it on drugs and fast ladies. How he finally hits bottom and heads back home. He's feeling like a failure but his father is ecstatic to see him back. The father throws his arms around him, hugs him, and throws a party for him like nothing happened. The son is overwhelmed by his father's unconditional love.

DOING TIME

I tell the sad inmate with the twirly mustache that this parable is a picture of what God is really like. And *he's not like us. His* love is unconditional. *His* mercy is without limits. It's really the parable of the prodigal father—a father almost foolishly generous with his mercy, no matter how far we stray.

As I say these beautiful words to the poor con, I feel a catch in my throat and my eyes begin to well, for I struggle to believe them just like he does. And though I believe them, I do not always feel them. I was a natural. How could God forgive *me* for leaving the priesthood? How could he forgive me for bringing such shame and pain on my family? And for scandalizing my students who had me on such a pedestal, and for abandoning the people I had instructed and baptized and absolved for over eleven years? How?

My guilt was like a private wound I tried to heal by running from the past. My running took the form of work—at the only place I was able to find a job: Raychem, a high-tech company growing 40 percent a year. I couldn't find a teaching position in religion, so I was forced to trade the academic leisure of the University of San Francisco (USF) for the pressure of Silicon Valley.

I was still a priest in my own mind and guiltily confessed to everyone that I had been, so I was not so conscious of that drop in status. I was no longer a successful college professor but a tyro in a strange new world.

I started running to succeed, I thought. Working in personnel, searching into the night for chemical engineers and PhDs to recruit. But my innards were churning with unresolved guilt. I was really running to escape the relentless dialogue in my conscience. At moments, it was like watching a tennis match, with my soul as the prize, wondering which player would win. My anxiety kept rising, the blood pinging against my skin like a million tiny bubbles. Then I cracked.

It took the form of soaking sweats at night and paralyzing headaches in the day. It was mononucleosis with hepatitis. But the exhaustion lingered with depression. My internist informed me bluntly: "Your red blood cells are back. You're fine. I think it's all in your head. Is it guilt or something? I think you need a shrink."

I was staggered by his suggestion. My whole life may have fallen apart but my *mind*? Was I cracking up? I feared losing control of my heretofore disciplined life, jumping into the white-water rapids of my emotions, not knowing where the rapids would take me.

I was referred, ironically, to a Doctor Comfort out of Stanford who helped me get in touch with my feelings. On one level, I was still considering returning to the priesthood. I still felt called, still heard the bugle blowing in the back of my mind. I loved being a priest. And the Jesuits at USF, who had kindly taken me in after I left Los Angeles, told me I was one of the two or three most popular professors on campus. They wanted me to stay. But I had struggled for years with my vow of celibacy, and I was demoralized. The priesthood is a beautiful life but a lonely one.

The summer before the "winter of my discontent," I met the woman who would become my future wife. Margie was a nun working in the inner city but her religious community was about to be suppressed. The sisters were too progressive, too feminist, too "Vatican II" for the cardinal. For both of us it was love at first sight. But she couldn't make the same decision to leave as I had, because her mother, who was dying of cancer, would be crushed. Then I couldn't decide. Half of me at least wished I could still be a priest. I missed God.

Then Margie's mother died, her religious community was dissolved, and she was no longer bound by her vows. She wanted me to make a decision. Two days after Christmas we were married.

6
THE "HISTORICAL JESUS"

One Sunday morning, Phil, the sharp, barrel-chested sacristan, informs me in his husky, low-key voice that San Quentin College needs someone to teach a New Testament course on Jesus. Phil could pass for the heavy in a Western, but he is a singularly bright and pious lifer who deeply repents a quick-tempered action of his teens. He is not and never has been a hardened criminal. His informing me of the opening is his way of asking me to seek the job. I reflect on all the hard work preparing a new course at the college level can be. It's thirty years since I taught theology at the University of San Francisco. But the thought of teaching a college course at the Q excites me and shines up my academic ego.

I run down Sean McPhetridge, the elusive community resources director who coordinates the college program on his own time, and I get the job. The absence of other applicants doesn't hurt.

San Quentin College is a two-year program that Earl Smith, the Protestant chaplain, helped start. It is accredited through Patten Bible College in Oakland, which helps explain a handful of required Bible courses. Now, however, most of the faculty come from the University of California at Berkeley. The professor who taught the Jesus course the previous year is chairman of the religion department of UC Davis. Phil tells me that the course shook the faith of some prisoners. I call last year's professor on the phone and he is very helpful. "The students are at the level of my students at UC." That may have been true of his first class; it won't be true of mine.

Our class starts in June. So I have two months to get ready. I drop the novel I am rewriting and take on the historical Jesus. It is a rich field of inquiry that concerns the most argued-about person in history. "Who do men say that I am?" Jesus once asked, and the question does not go away. I check out the sources once more with scholar friends. And shortly I am into John Meier's magisterial work in the Anchor Bible Series, *A Marginal Jew,* his multivolume study of the "historical Jesus," that is, what we can know about Jesus from history itself. Then Raymond Brown, the great New Testament scholar. C. H. Dodd and Joachim Jeremias on the parables. The Jerome Biblical Commentary. And so on, until I am finally back from the intellectually dead. It is quietly exciting to sense my mind coming alive again in the field I love. I feel finger-snapping smart again, like Michael Jordan returning after thirty years to regain his touch.

The first night in June I get to the prison early. The classroom—one of three in the basement of the ancient brick education building (education was once a high priority at the prison)—has the same grimy, spiritless, cream concrete walls as in the cellblocks. It is crammed with twenty scarred desks before a tired lectern. Behind the lectern—a whiteboard with a dead marker and the unerasable traces of a hundred classes. The men will feel right at home. What little education most prisoners have received (60 percent of all prisoners cannot read or write) has been in rundown, poorly equipped classrooms. I look out at the summer sunset reaching through the large industrial windows and realize I will be "blinded by the light," so to speak, as I lecture.

Three TAs, teaching assistants, arrive: Janet, a Catholic activist friend, Peace Corps veteran, and Harvard English major; Steve, a bright, open, graduate student in astronomy at UC Berkeley, who tells me right up front: "I'm an agnostic"; and Maureen, a Catholic woman and PhD in her fifties, who is working on a theology degree at the Graduate Theological Union while she teaches statistics at Berkeley. The job of the TA is to help the students outside of class—with the lectures, reading assignments, and papers—one other night during the week. God knows they will need it. Most of them have prison jobs (thirty hours a week; $100 a month) so their time is limited. Study conditions can be difficult (rock music on the tier, their half-deaf cellie in the bunk above, watching TV), and their educational backgrounds are minimal if not primitive. They are the products of the worst school systems in California. But the smarts are there and the desire. And like many others, I will fall in love with these guys. If your heart is pumping blood you've got to.

My students drift in. I welcome them, trying to catch their names, but their diction is not crisp, my hearing can be muddy, and some have three-word Islamic names. The class is filled with twenty-two men identically dressed in blue jeans and blue denim shirts. More than half the class is Black, along with a few whites, a couple of Native Americans, Asians, and Latinos. All but one of the Blacks, who is from Africa or the Islands, sit on the left side of the classroom. I struggle to get some names straight. Names that aren't Joe or Mike but Alghazal or Al Basar. To my eyes, some of the men—muscular, overweight, broad smiles—look alike. It becomes almost a class joke but they are extremely good-natured about it. I am embarrassed because I want to give them the respect they deserve—to be called by their proper names.

I study their large, well-muscled bodies—prisons run on starch and push-ups in the cells—and look into their curious, expectant faces. I remember that most of them are lifers who have probably killed somebody and could snap my neck with one hand tied behind their back. There is no guard anywhere around. Then I begin.

I tell them I'm an expriest, a former college professor, and a believer. I tell them some scholars say the only thing we can know about Jesus that is reliable is through history itself, not the gospels, and that isn't very much; that is, it isn't "scientific history." At the other extreme, some scholars say that the only Christ that is "real" for a Christian is the risen Christ, known though faith. In the middle are those who say we must learn everything we can about Christ from history, as best as we can two-thousand years later, while at the same time remembering that, for a believer, the Christ of faith—the risen and present Christ we experience through faith—is the "real" Jesus, not a person deliberately "constructed" from historical facts.

The first night I lay out the world that Jesus entered so long ago, a world Hellenized by Alexander, run by the Romans, yet Jewish at its core from Abraham, Moses, and the prophets. At that time, it was tense with political religious parties: Pharisees, Sadducees, Essenes, and Zealots. The second night we examine our prime source for Jesus—the Bible, especially the New Testament—and how and when it came to be. That is, who decided which books were inspired by the Holy Spirit and which were apocryphal. I inform them that Saint Athanasius, the Bishop of Alexandria, decided the canon of the New Testament in his Easter letter of 367 AD. There were scrolls and fragments, but the Bible as we know it didn't exist yet and was unknown as such by the common man who was illiterate.

As I say these things, I am intensely conscious of their widening eyes and the gulf between myself and many of my students. Most of them are Fundamentalists, who hold to the literal interpretation of the scriptures. I am thinking of the story about the teacher applying for a teaching job in the South. He tells the interviewer, "Some say the earth is round, some say it's flat. I'm a flat man myself but I can teach it either way." I can't. Along with recent popes and mainstream scripture scholars, both Protestant and Catholic, I teach that the scriptures include a range of literary forms—history, myth, poetry, sayings, proverbs, and so on. Every line, therefore, is not to be taken literally. But I do not hammer the differences home. Rather, I report what the better scholars, believers, and unbelievers of the "inspired word" hold concerning a given text. For example, Raymond Brown explains why the infancy narratives of Matthew and Luke are so different. (Mark and John don't even have one.) Colorful characters and stunning incidents are missing from one account or the other and are almost contradictory (the star, the wicked king, the wise men, the shepherds, the inn). The gospels are primarily faith testimonies, and the intent of the evangelists is to reach their respective audiences with a theological message about Jesus, not twentieth-century scientific history. How could the wonder and majesty of God becoming man be communicated more beautifully than in the unforgettable accounts of Matthew and Luke?

From time to time there are tightening foreheads and quizzical looks, and I can't miss the gilt-edged Bibles with Post-it tabs on some desks. But my students seem to trust me, even though I explain certain texts in new and potentially disturbing ways, because, obviously, I believe.

One Asian student, a former Catholic, is now a Funda-mentalist and a "prison minister." He rarely smiles or laughs at my jokes and his demeanor is generally grim. He has some bitter feelings toward the church, I'm told. Another, an Anglo, regularly raises provocative, skeptical, even snide questions in class. He sounds like the village atheist. I patiently and perhaps too lengthily answer his questions. "There is no such thing as a dumb question," I say at the start of the course. The rest of the class laughs or groans when he raises questions. They find him disruptive, time-consuming, and nasty. They tell me, "Ignore him." Ironically, I give him an A on his first paper. It's excellent. His second paper is obviously not up to the first, and he lashes out at me at the end for "preaching." I worry about that. I have a charismatic lecture style, but I work hard to be fair and objective while making my personal opinions clear. I sample a range of students. They shake their heads and say, "He's full of it." Phil, another student, tells me, "His mother goes to Mass and communion every morning and he's still rebelling." Cons don't miss a trick when it comes to their peers. A fellow con might as well be a flea under a microscope.

In typical prison fashion, the three-hour class scheduled to start at 6:30 p.m. never starts on Pacific Standard Time. It starts on "prison time," another phrase for "late" due to lockdowns, once an attempted break, count-offs, or seemingly any arbitrary thing. So, at 7 or 7:30 p.m. the students drift in. The men are older—thirties, forties, fifties—and though not brilliant, they are capable and eager to learn. As I correct the first assigned paper it becomes clear they do not know how to write one; that is, a paper with a thesis, arguments, citations from lecture notes, texts, commentaries, and a conclusion. I tell them how to write a paper, then give examples and pass around a model of what I want. No more stream of consciousness or feelings about God. Research and scholarship. The second set of papers—with much help from Wendy, Steve, and Maureen, the TAs—is excellent. They get used to strange concepts like Bultmann's "realized eschatology" and "the messianic secret." And they get smarter by the week.

At moments, like in a freeze frame, I catch the sadness, resignation, and deferred hope in their eyes; another death in the family or funeral they couldn't attend or child's birthday missed. By the end of the course, I have learned much more from them than they have from me. Their easy warmth and closeness to the scriptures and their belief in Jesus is as touching as anything I have ever encountered.

At the completion of the final exam in late August, the TAs—Wendy, Steve and Maureen—and I bid our students goodbye then share our thoughts. We have bonded with these men. We have experienced their warm humanity, their humor, their indomitable spirit. We wish they were free. In a way, we hate to see the class end and agree we are much changed because of it.

Steve, a delightfully positive young man, tells me, before he leaves, he would like to be a TA for any class I teach. Then he adds, "Maybe we could teach a faith-science class together." I tell him, "I would like that."

7

ROME, VENICE, AND THE DEATH PENALTY

Within days, I finish correcting exams and submit my grades to the college program's administration. It's been a satisfying but grueling few months preparing and delivering the course lectures. I need a break. The next day my second wife, Patty, and I catch a plane to visit Rome and Venice.

A trip to Italy is sunny—if not in weather, then certainly in spirit. Beauty, laughter, and good red wine. Balmy nights, full moons, and coins in a fountain. But to me, Italy's sunniness is bittersweet. Fifteen years ago, my first wife died suddenly and tragically of breast cancer. Margie had had a taste for beauty and an irrepressible zest for life. A scripture scholar who knew her wrote: "Margie was the sunniest person I ever met in a well-traveled life." That's the word: *sunniest.* When she died, the sunniness was gone, and I was devastated.

In time I met and married my beloved Patty, and now we are in the sunny, fantasy world of Rome and Venice, staying with her widowed aunt on the Via Veneto, a stone's throw from the Borghese Gardens. Olga is a ball of energy, intelligence, and culture. She is also a famous attorney (Gore Vidal, her cousin, is a client), an incomparable host, and, most important, fun.

Olga and Italy—I believe this is what Hilaire Belloc was thinking when, in recounting a vinous pilgrimage from London, reeled off this quatrain:

DOING TIME

In Catholic countries of sunny clime
There's always laughter and good red wine.
At least I have always found it so.
Benedicamus Domino.

Patty and I happily walk the stone-cobbled streets to "feel" the city. We stop at the Church of Santa Maria della Vittoria. On a side altar on the left is Bernini's breathtaking *St. Teresa in Ecstasy.* I stare at the amazing sculpture until its beautiful transcendence runs through me like a shiver. Teresa's finger is alive, her eyes are in heaven.

We also see an exhibit of Botticelli's squiggly brown pen sketches of each canto of Dante's *Divina Comedia:* characters Dante had dispatched to hell to suffer various well-deserved torments. Of course, I am made to remember my cons at the various levels of hell that comprise the Q. The men may not be planted upside down in rock, or lying face up in a ring of burning sand under a fiery rain, but they are still in hell. The Q is raw reality, squared and compounded. A harsh world of clanging cell doors, hard looks, brusque commands, and hope nurtured not too carefully for fear of it cratering in disappointment as so many times. I feel a twinge of guilt luxuriating in the balmy Roman night, a free man.

Later, I am reminded that one of the first visits John XXIII made after becoming pope was to Regina Coeli prison in Rome. Popes had not ventured outside the Vatican for centuries, and here was good Pope John embracing and empathizing with prisoners as tears fell down the cheeks of reporters, TV cameramen, and prisoners alike. He told them humbly: "I come from poor people. There are only three ways of losing money in Italy: farming, gambling, and women. My father chose the least interesting way. One of my brothers was caught poaching; an uncle did time. These are the things that happen to poor people. But we are all children of God. And I am Joseph, your brother." Pope John was referring, of course, to Joseph in Egypt. Giuseppe, Joseph, was the pope's middle name.

Maybe that is why I work with prisoners—the most despised and wretched in society. They are Christ's poor. The ones for whom he felt such compassion. What I give them is minimal. What they give me has no price. I feel I am touching Christ in their presence and, being poor, few of them have traveled to faraway places. Rome is just a word or a picture on a postcard. To give you an idea, McManus once had this conversation with an inmate:

"I'm going to Dublin for my vacation," McManus said.

"Where is that?" the inmate asked.

"It's far, far away."

"How long is it by bus?"

Patty and I travel from Rome to Venice. We observe the furrowed farmlands and the quaint, sharply-pitched roofs on the earth-toned rectangular houses. We take the water-taxi on the bustling Grand Canal past lovers in gondolas and past seemingly water-based mansions. Then we meander the labyrinthine alleyways to our first destination. As the rays of the descending sun stream over a flutter of birds and long lines of tourists, we are astonished once more by the magical piazza and Church of San Marco: Spires and domes and colored glass. Horses jumping off the facade. Stony saints fixed in piety. The dark sacredness inside. We move on to the palace of the doges, who were the chief magistrates in Venice. In the Grand Council chamber is Tintoretto's masterpiece, *Paradise* over the doges' throne. But as we walk the Bridge of Sighs *(Ponte dei Sospiri)*, connecting the doges' palace with a prison,

DOING TIME

I am again thinking of the Q. The "sighs" were the lamentations of prisoners crossing the bridge to their execution. The dark, cramped cells are dungeon-quality but not much worse than today.

The next day, we visit the School of San Rocco, which contains fifty-six extraordinary canvasses by Tintoretto. An Englishman, looking like a world-weary Graham Greene and obviously knowledgeable, points to the sweeping crucifixion scene directly in front of us and says quietly to his friends: "This is one of the five great paintings in the world." Our attention perks up after a long, touristy day. Patty and I examine the painting's scope and detail with greater diligence. The Englishman is right. The painting is magnificent. You are actually there on Calvary: the vivid execution scene under the somber sky, the sight of Christ hanging by nails between two thieves. The Q. Death Row. The death penalty.

Back in Rome, we take the subway to the Vatican and stumble into a "private audience" with Pope John Paul II and fifty-thousand people. They are from many small towns in Italy, drawn to honor this special "living saint." From the shade of Bernini's great colonnade, I can see the huge TV screen on which John Paul's image is projected. His advancing Parkinson's disease is a shock. He looks like a hunchback, draped over the mike to address the crowd from his chair in the morning sunshine. His voice is the groan of a drunk or a stroke victim. He is only a shell and an echo—though a gutsy one—of the once-athletic, vigorous young pope.

John Paul has been very progressive in many areas despite his conservative tag; one of those areas is the death penalty, which he sees as part of "the culture of death." He writes: "The dignity of human life must never be taken away, even in the case of someone who has done great evil. I renew the appeal for a consensus to end the death penalty which is both cruel and unnecessary."

Justice Scalia, a conservative Catholic, dismissed the pope's plea by saying "he couldn't find it in the tradition" (the early fathers of the church, Augustine, Thomas, and others). It would seem that Scalia does not consider the "Christ part" of the tradition. "If you do not forgive others your Father will not forgive you." Scalia's dismissal of the pope's cause was so casual, he seemed almost enthusiastic about capital punishment. It reminds me of William Buckley's infamous response to John XXIII's encyclical on the duty of the rich nations to share their wealth with the poor: *"Mater si, Magistra no."* No pope is going to tell the rich what to do with their riches. For Scalia and Buckley, when it comes to crunch time, the right-wing agenda and the trickle-down philosophy have clear precedence over Jesus' scandalous gospel: "Woe to you rich."

It strikes me that these men are apologists for the rich— and the rich, as Belloc once said, "are the scum of the earth in every generation." I believe that wealth, or the desire for it, and the death penalty are ultimately connected. How?

In a society where money is the measure of all things, wealth is a screen against and a blindness toward those without it. The human race shrinks down to that small percent of people who possess it. All others are outside the rich man's purview or ability to understand. Society is better off when the criminal element is off the streets or is dead. "Criminal element" is a code word for "poor," which means brown-skinned or Black. They are the ones who spend their lives in prison or die by lethal injection. The life of the rich is valuable life; the life of the poor is not. So, the rich live oblivious to the poor.

An extreme example is El Salvador. Seventy-thousand desperately poor, including a bishop and many priests and nuns, were slaughtered by the handful of rich families who run the country. Why? Justice was a threat to their riches. Liberation theologians in Latin America speak of false idols replacing the true God. The first is wealth. The second is national security to protect the wealth. In El Salvador, national security was the idol used to justify the murder of seventy-thousand citizens.

Before we leave Rome, we discuss the death penalty with Olga. Italy, along with the rest of the European Union, has outlawed the practice. It was Albert Camus, the existentialist, who led the cause in the years following World War II. After fifty million dead, he asked, "Do we really need to perpetuate the killing process?"

8
A GAY AT THE Q

As I make my way through the concrete yard from Donner to West Block, the prisoners strike me as passive, phlegmatic, dopey-looking, or burned-out from drugs and despair. They are obviously repeaters, drying out on taxpayers' dollars. Some cons see it as the rhythm of their life. Their thread of hope is spiderweb-fine. But occasionally there is a superbright and fascinating con in the yard. This morning one recognizes me as I wade through a sea of men with byzantine tattoos, butt-tough faces, and "no future" looks in their eyes. He was at my communion service yesterday. His name is Reggie and he is in the Q for stalking his former lover. Red-haired and blue-eyed, with a slightly high-strung, thin-skinned nervousness about him, he is charming and articulate. A graduate of a top five high-tech university. We lean into each other against the noise and the constantly passing inmates. He is obviously comfortable with a priest and likes being a Catholic. He is also sexually obsessive. So, he wants to do parole, in a few months, five-hundred miles away from San Francisco and his gay lover, the "stalkee."

"What if the parole department won't let you?" Parole departments have been burned so many times that, I suppose, they begin to think: *Punishment, not reform. Parolees are no good.*

Reggie purses his lips. Reflects for a minute.

"Well, I hate to say it but I'm actually comfortable here—outside of the racism. The food is good. I have a beautiful view of Mount Tamalpais, I can't stalk my lover and, frankly, there's a lot of good-looking guys around here."

I smile at the irony and the honesty but he doesn't notice, he is so absorbed in his anxiety. We pray in the open air and crowds of inmates, milling and gaping as they pass in the yard. Praying publicly in prison is part of the culture. There's no privacy. You're naked in the shower. Together you pray in the yard. I give him communion.

How does homosexuality fit at the Q? Is it dangerous? Is a homosexual placed in protective custody—the SHU: Secure Housing Unit? No, unless he is victimized or stalked by another prisoner. From time to time, the prisoners allude to "he-ing and he-ing."

McManus says, "How would they do it? The guards lock them in their cells. They are under steady surveillance."

Deacon George answers, "Quickly."

In Donner, I encounter a string of Latinos in cell after cell. Prisoners in the cells tend to come in short stretches of similarity: Latinos or Anglos. Diversity is not high in the prison culture. Blacks are calling out or shouting, trying to get a phone call out of volunteers. (It's against the rules for a brown card.) The Latinos are more passive, subdued, isolated by language along with everything else. One prisoner told me he had such problems with language at his trial, he thought he had been sentenced to seven years. It wasn't until a guard called him a "lifer" that he realized the full impact of his fate.

This morning the Latinos look particularly forlorn. I start talking to José. He is a nice young man in his late twenties. So gentle, I wonder what he did to get here. Drugs, of course. Maybe more. Maybe he's less innocent than he appears or maybe just weak like the rest of us. He is a *Catolico*.

I ask him: "Do you pray?"

He answers like a child: "How to pray?"

He gives me pause. Doesn't everyone know how to pray? But the more I think about it, maybe they don't. Jesus had to tell the apostles: "Don't babble like the pagans do." Then he taught them the Our Father. So, I do the same. José and I touch fingertips through the mesh on the bars. I lead him slowly line by line and he repeats after me: *Our Father. Our Father. In Heaven. In Heaven. May your name be held holy.* May your name....The great mystic Teresa of Avila would fall into ecstasy with the words *Our Father.* José and I don't quite but we pray hard. Earnestly. Concentrating, heads bowed. We do not achieve ecstasy—only a passing mystical moment or two in this noisy, hellish place. At the end, I test José's contrition and his faith in the Eucharist, as he asked me to receive. I take the host from the gold pyx in the small black case hanging from my neck. *Behold the Lamb of God.* Through the narrow gap at the top corner of the cell door, I hand Jesus in the bread to José. *Cuerpo de Christo.* José takes the bread between two fingers and feeds on Jesus. Together we thank the Lord and ask him to bless everyone on the tier. I jot his name down on the back of an envelope, but he probably will be transferred by next week—or deported.

Prisoners in the reception center are in here mostly for drugs, crimes related to drug use, and parole violations. Their ignorance of the faith is vast and deep, and their sacramental practice after baptism minimal as a rule. Receiving the Eucharist can easily be an act of superstition like a Black Baptist wearing a rosary around his neck—which so many do. But faith is closer to superstition than reason, I remind myself. And that incarnational sense of God's presence in created things—God in the man Jesus, grace in the water of baptism, power in the relic—is a very Catholic notion. If a prisoner does not believe or is not ready to receive, he tells you so. But if he is sorry for his sins at this moment and desires Jesus, who am I to deny him? It may be his last touch with the church for a long time. One of the axioms in sacramental theology is *sacramenta propter homines:* people weren't made for the sacraments; the sacraments were made for people. And though we often don't acknowledge it, every inmate is a person too.

9
A CRUEL JOKE

For a lifer, the Q often seems like the kingdom of the abandoned run by the indifferent. They've locked you up and thrown away the key. The caretakers of the kingdom take notice only when you step out of expected behavior.

DOING TIME

One day, a couple of lifers are joking and laughing out loud about some prison inanity.

A guard comes up: "What are you guys laughing about? You're in prison. You're not supposed to be having fun."

A lifer is seldom paroled, and so feels abandoned by society and eventually by the law of the land itself.

These dark thoughts are in my head this week because Dominic, part of "the family"—McManus, Father Peter Togñi, Deacon George, and me—is going before the board of prisons terms—the parole board.

When I first encountered Dominic, a ruggedly handsome, curly haired "Portagee," he would joke and kid around. His smile would quickly ignite a throaty rumble of a laugh and slurry of words accented from his immigrant roots. He grew to trust me and got serious one day. He told me he was from a rough patch in the East Bay. When he first came to the Q he was a scrawny kid but he soon buffed up—a necessity in a place where the smallest biceps are fifteen inches and weakness is the only sin. Then he told me what put him here.

"I got laid off and couldn't find a job. So, I hook up with four other guys on the block. It's a tough block. I'm runnin' with them a couple of months and they decide to kidnap this rich guy's daughter. I'm broke and stupid so I go along. The cops catch us the next day."

"What about the girl?"

"Nobody touched her. The DA made a deal with Vasco, the leader. Vasco fingers me as the guy behind the whole thing. I'm with them two months. They've been doin' bad for two years!"

"Why couldn't you fight it?"

"Vasco threatened to hurt my family if I fingered him."

I shake my head.

"Yeah. So, the judge gave me seven-to-life and told my parents, 'He'll be free in seven years.' That was seventeen years ago. My parents think I must be doin' something wrong inside."

"What about the other guys?"

"They got out in five. Hey, don't get me wrong. I did something terrible and I should be punished *but* it doesn't seem fair—*and* the judge said seven."

I note the pain of remembering in Dominic's eyes. He's the fall guy in a noir film.

I am feeling the anxiety and sweaty-handed hope Dominic must be feeling because he is coming up once more before the parole board. He has a perfect record in prison: Not one blemish in seventeen years. The highest references from officers he has worked under: A psychiatric evaluation that says he represents no risk to society upon release. Exceptional. He has been up for parole and denied seven times in seven years and all of this was true each time. It's hard because the heart of Dominic's life is hope.

Many parole boards across the country do not believe in rehabilitation—in particular for those who commit serious crimes and for lifers—as firmly as the prisoners believe they should. I heard that a prisoner sued the Q for exactly those reasons and that the judge demanded a review of parole policies. So maybe, every man tells himself, maybe there is the tiniest possibility that the board will see *his* case in a different, more positive light this time. Maybe the board will read the earnestness in his eyes or sense the change in his heart. And maybe, at the least, the board will say that he's made progress. Then maybe, next time. Thus, Dominic hopes.

The end of the week, I spot Dominic staring through the steel fence, looking down at the men in the yard far below: his head down, his hands jammed in his denim jacket, his face a hundred years older.

"I told 'em I been doin' good for seventeen years," he says. "No 115s [write-ups], no problems. I can't do any better. I know I did a terrible thing, but I've paid for it. I'm doin' my best."

As we stand in the sunshine, Deacon George comes by on the way to North Block. He stops.

"I heard, Dommie," he says succinctly and waits to listen. That's the heart of what we do: we listen. Who else does an inmate have to talk to? Disclosing is weakness and vulnerability with anyone else.

"*Seven times* I go to the board," Dominic says, squeezing the anger from his fist. "*Seven times* I got a perfect record. They say, 'You a model prisoner. But your crime's not paid for yet.' I do everything they say. They turn me down." His shoulders sag.

"I grew up in a tough neighborhood," he continues, almost on the verge of tears, but he won't cry. Prisoners never do. Lots of fear. "You tell nobody nothin'. You act tough with everybody. The only way you survive. You show weakness and you go down. A victim." His harsh voice softens. "But here at the Q, Father O'Neill, Father McManus, and you, George—you teach me to open up my heart. I learn to forgive. In my heart, I'm grateful to God. I experience love for the first time, *first* time." He makes the point with a shaking finger.

It's a tender moment worth all the hours standing outside the cells on the hard concrete tiers wondering if you're making a difference, doing any good. I wish the parole board could observe him right now. It's a moment of truth. Dominic knows he is not the same man who entered the Q. After seventeen years you can't be.

George and I continue on our ways when Dominic leaves. As George breaks off and heads toward North Block, I continue under the vast tin-roofed upper yard.

I stop to strike up a conversation with a mainliner in his denim jacket and jeans. The few strands of silvering hair don't quite cover his sunburned dome. There's a hard, resigned look in his eyes that says he's been here a long time; they'll probably carry him out of here. I mention Dominic. There's an instinctive empathy for anyone going before the board, along with hope that the right decision might start a trend. But not today. The mainliner has already heard the news. He tosses a cigarette he has smoked to the nub.

"I heard the parole board is made up of law-enforcement officers and victims of crime," the mainliner says. "How would you like a jury of those people if your life was hanging on it?"

I stay silent. He needs to vent and is getting red-faced just talking about it. He doesn't look healthy. He smokes and eats all that starch in the prison diet. I can tell he's been through the "public whipping" a few times himself.

He continues: "I even heard the DAs share their secrets with each other to use at parole hearings. Tips on how to keep us from getting out. Even made up a manual. You ever hear that?"

"No," I said. "I didn't."

"The guys think they know why. More prisoners are more work. More work is more overtime. *And* more work is more job security."

He curses all of them.

Most men doing time—hard time—are grim realists or cynics about getting out. They know the cards are stacked against them.

In 1988, Willie Horton, a prisoner on furlough, tortured and raped a young couple. He never should have been released.

But in the shallow world of sound bites, images, and montage, his murders meant that the whole system across the country had been "soft on crime." Since then, it's the kiss of death for any person or group to be soft on crime.

No parole makes no sense and goes against all the research as well as the experience of prison administrators. The media, which loves crime and violence, has convinced the masses that all criminals are intrinsically vicious, so punishment is the only answer. *Punish, punish, punish.* But it's a very dangerous policy. A prison is already a terrible place where men crowded into small cages live in fear and violence. Without some degree of the humane, the lives of the guards are endangered, prisoners are unmanageable, and rehabilitation for those who *are* released is impossible.

America's prison system emphasizes punishment, not rehabilitation, even though that policy is draining desperately needed money from our schools and communities. Even the more relaxed Q supports rehabilitation through the use of free community resources *only*. Not a dime from the state. Shortly after I finished teaching my course on "The Historical Jesus," Sean McPhetridge, who was running the program in his spare time as director of community resources, resigned. Among other things, there was no budget for it and no effort to build additional needed classrooms. As he left, he told me: "After seven years it got to me. I think I'm the only one at the Q who believes in rehabilitation."

The people in the tony neighborhood five miles down the road have the impression it is a scary place (parts of it are) full of scary men (some are). That every next man is ready to rape or kill anyone who comes through the East Gate. When someone does nervously enter the prison for the first time, they are invariably surprised to find that men who have killed someone with a knife or their bare hands are human beings like them-selves. Sister Helen Prejean is an anti-death penalty activist and author of *Dead Man Walking*. She says, "An evil act does not make a man evil." The recidivism rate of killers is the low-est in the prison. It shouldn't be surprising. A man does one terrible thing, then has twenty or thirty years to think about it—every day. Ironically, you are less likely to be hurt by an aging lifer than by a short-termer brutalized by the prison system since his teens, or a druggie thug in his late twenties who hasn't done real time yet.

McManus, Deacon George, and Earl Smith, the Protestant chaplain, are the first to say when a prisoner is not quite ready for the streets. All the perfect behavior inside may cover up an unresolved anger streak—the kind that can become instantly lethal—or a proneness to violence or a prison-controlled addiction. So, when McManus or Deacon George even an indifferent guard says Dominic's ready, you know he is. And there are more than a few Dominics inside who are.

10

TOO MUCH CHAMPAGNE

Monday morning again. I'm trolling the tiers of Alpine looking for business, looking for someone gripping the prison bars too tightly and staring at me, silently asking me to talk to them. It's December-cool outside with the damp breezes off the Bay, but many of the men are stripped to the waist or their white Skivvies. So many large bodies are squeezed into this cellblock—twice its capacity—that it's almost always too hot or stifling, especially on the upper tiers. The cells are so dark and dingy it's hard to make out the beat, bearded, pocked, and scarred faces of the Blacks, browns, or whites inside. So many have that resigned, low-gear look in their eyes and have stayed at the Q so many times that it's easy to think of them as life's losers. Black, brown, or white trash. But I see them as the wounded, the collateral damage of a dysfunctional family: the human family.

I listen, talk, and pray with several Blacks. I test my Spanish with a cell of Michoacán braceros, migrant workers from Mexico here on temporary permits. It fails. Their Spanish is mushy—not Castilian crisp—and braceros are not very verbal. I have a passing thought of going to Cochabamba in Bolivia to improve my Spanish. But a Maryknoll missionary tells me it's a waste of time after the age of fifty.

About to leave the block, I spot a large Black man who, even in the darkness, has a certain presence about him. Our eyes engage through the black mesh and bars. I can barely make out his features at first. My eyes become accustomed to the dark.

"Hi. What's your name?"

"Danny O'Brien."

I smile to myself. Danny O'Brien. Maybe it's the cell but he's the blackest dude I've seen all day. "Drugs and alcohol?"

"I had a little too much one night."

"You're in deep trouble. You're Black *and* Irish, and neither one can drink."

He laughs. "But I don't have a drinking problem."

"What got you here?"

"One night I had a little champagne. I really like champagne."

"How much?"

"Six bottles." Straight-faced.

"That's a lot."

"Naw," he says, shaking his head. "It wasn't that. I do that all the time. It was the weed my girl gave me."

"But how did you get in here?"

"They said I tried to choke her but I don't remember anything."

"I guess you wouldn't."

He's not only into denial, he's into amnesia. Denial is big at the Q, and now I realize it's because they weren't even conscious when they did it—whatever it was.

"How long you in for?"

"My attorney says Christmas."

"You going to do champagne again?"

He shrugs. "I'm in rip-rap music in LA. Everyone does booze and drugs in rip-rap."

"You better get a new girl then."

I move down the tier and stop at a wasted-looking white man clinging to the bars of his cell. He says his mother is dying and he needs the chaplain's help to make a phone call. The "dying mother" is the excuse inmates frequently use in the reception center to be able to phone out. McManus and Deacon George check out "dying mothers" and deaths and find out they're not true a large part of the time. Men in blue denim on the mainline have weekly phone privileges but men in the reception center—there sometimes for four-to-six months—have none except for an emergency like a dying mother. When they do get to call, the home phone is often out of service because the dying mother or the wife with the baby can't pay the bill with the breadwinner in the Q. But as this man talks, I can tell he's not conning me. There's something too desperate, too real about him. Then he tells me he has AIDS. I can see it before he tells me.

He's a Nazarene but "leans" toward being a Catholic. I tell him it doesn't matter. A prison is like a home for the dying, and when people are dying, God is more important than creeds, Mother Teresa says. You listen and you try to comfort. I tell him he's important, more important than lots of people outside. *I was in prison and you visited me.*

Heading back to the chapel, I spot Reggie, the gay stalker, in the lower yard outside the gym. Through white wisps of clouds, I can see magnificent Mount Tamalpais watching over the Q and stripped-down Blacks playing a pickup game of hoops, glistening with sweat even in the faint sun. I love to watch basketball, the fluid moves to the bucket. None of the inmates can hit from outside but they can take it down the pipe. Playground ball. I wonder for a moment how many of them "just missed" getting on a college or even an NBA team early on. They've got the size and the quickness and the gristle. All they lack is discipline—the same as in their lives.

Reggie is getting out just before Christmas, so he should be up, but he looks down. He already told me he wants to be released in another county because the object of his obsession is in San Francisco. He's in his mind as he talks, not looking at me or at anyone. He's anguished, desperate—because 99 percent of the time the bureaucracy says no to any such request. Reggie is smart. He's gotten the law books out of the library and found that, by law, a parole officer cannot release a prisoner into an area that is likely to lead him into his crime again. Reggie is also scared. That's the law, but parole officers know, by experience, that the farther away geographically that a parolee is from them, the more likely it is he'll get in trouble. Even so, it strikes me as slightly absurd that a prisoner is fighting desperately to avoid "the occasion of sin" that got him into the Q in the first place—and isn't allowed to.

Reggie has already spent $2,000 on a lawyer who did nothing for him, a common complaint. Taking on the system by himself feels like taking on the world. Especially when, from the outside, the system is a law unto itself.

Suddenly Reggie, who is high-spirited by nature, turns sunny. He is writing a children's story about a bad little boy who messes with a woman who turns out to be, a witch. She casts a spell on him and suddenly he is in an orange jumpsuit and his room is turned into a cell. Finally, the bad little boy in his orange jumpsuit and Q-like cell learns his lesson becomes a good little boy, and the witch releases him from his spell.

When Reggie finishes telling me his story, I turn Freudian, of course. Reggie is the boy and the witch must be his mother. Then again, Warden Jane is a woman. A recurring mother figure? But I explore none of this with Reggie. The big thing, I tell him, is to get it published.

My rounds, the chill in the air, the weak-sunned winter day have me thinking of Christmas. It's a biting sadness for the men at the Q not to be home for Christmas: the distance from loved ones, the absence of any kind of warmth, the reminder they've blown it again.

11
THE GUARDS

As the choir warms up on this cool January morning, and the men in orange jumpsuits begin to drift into the chapel for the Sunday communion service, I will turn to my big burly altar boy and ask: "What's your opinion of the guards?"

The very bright lifer with very definite opinions screws up his face and answers: "A prison is a terrible place. It's got serial killers, drug peddlers, molesters, wife abusers—and that's just the guards." I laugh at his Mark Twain humor. He smiles broadly, appreciated.

Later I survey an aging lifer from the Protestant chapel who's already been in over twenty years. Maybe it's a bad day for him, but his face hardens.

"Some of them are evil." He spits out the last word.

I ask him about his boss on his work duty, an officer I respect.

"Oh, he's a great guy."

Then he turns negative again: "There's a huge turnover in guards. A dozen a month. I've heard of misdemeanors, even felonies. *Honest.* Even with the money they make—and the overtime."

My first impression of the guards—other than the officer at the East Gate—was off-putting. Cool, brusque, tight-lipped to everyone except their fellow guards. The size of quite a few is imposing. Some could pass as defensive tackles for the 49ers.

One intense, shaggy-haired con rattles off "guard stories" like jokes. I can see the secret delight he takes in their sins and failings.

"Did you see that article where a union guy was indicted?"

"I didn't get to the paper this morning."

"Yeah. Bringing drugs into a prison."

"No kidding."

"That's nothing, though. Did you see where Charles Manson was indicted for the same thing?" Manson is the crazed messiah who inspired the murder of Sharon Tate and a few others.

"No."

"Manson is under *maximum security,*" the con says, his voice rising with indignation. "So where did *he* get the drugs?"

Every long-termer knows the stories. Recounting them is their favorite indoor sport. To them, it seems like a prison is outside the law and the sergeants run the army. In all fairness, even without guards, a prison would be a mean and danger-ous place. Most of the men at the Q are parole violators, drug-gies, alcoholics—not life-threatening. But some are murderers and rapists, some are occasionally violent, and some are a lit-tle wacko. You never know what will set them off. There are also some twisted people here who have a warped and malev-olent view of the world. Life here is about using people, get-ting yours. With such a philosophy the prisoners could be key Enron executives but they didn't go to the best schools. In fact, they often didn't go to school at all. They developed only their biceps, triceps, and pectorals. The flesh that isn't tattooed is hairy and twitching for action. Their bodies are lethal instru-ments. As McManus says, "This isn't overnight at the county jail. You have to do something *really, really* bad to get in here."

And then there are the gangs. In some ways the younger set of the Q form the meanest, toughest "junior-high" in the meanest part of the worst city you've ever seen. Fear, is always in the air. Why do some men join gangs? Protection against getting knifed. But there's a price for protection: it's called favors. Like carrying messages or drugs, going along with a rape or a knifing, lying to an officer. So the con is compro-mised or he risks doing additional time or not getting a break on a parole date—or getting a shiv in his back from another gang. So there's always tension in the air.

DOING TIME

The Blacks, of course, have their Crips and Bloods. But the most populous gangs now are Hispanic: the Norteños from the north and the Sureños from the south (LA mostly). The Sureños outnumber the Norteños five to one and are the toughest. One Sunday when I was new I looked over the heavily Hispanic congregation and asked: "How many of you are from LA?" The chapel was icy still. Nobody moved or raised a hand. After the communion service, my altar boy says, "If they raise their hand they could get hurt. Norteños versus Sureños is a kind of tong war—ready to break out at any time."

And then there are the skinheads. They come from the poor white side of society and may be meaner and more full of hatred than any group at the Q. They shave their heads, give me a loveless eye as I pass in the yard, and stick tightly to their own. Recently, the whole prison was locked down because some guy in Badger—Level 3 and 4 cellblocks, which are maximum security—had his throat slit by a skinhead. The guy made it a practice to be friendly with Blacks as well as whites. The skinheads warned him: "Stick with your own people." He kept socializing. One day a skinhead approached and asked him for a cigarette. As the friendly guy reached into his pocket, a second skinhead pinned his arm and the first sliced his throat. The blade was a metal piece from a bunk bed sharpened to a razor's edge. The guy barely survived but after much loss of blood.

Once an alcohol-ravaged inmate confided to me in a whisper through the bars that his cellie, who had *white racist* tattooed on his biceps, was intimidating him, trying to get him to "do things." The inmate was older and frail and frightened. I immediately told the officer in charge, who had him moved to another cellblock in minutes. Guards are good about that.

Any gang—Crips, Bloods, Norteños, Sureños—can trigger violence at any time. Lockdowns—men confined to their cells for days without yard breaks—happen almost once a month. Most are racist at root. So, again, there's tension in the air. A guy squeezes into the food line ahead of you and sometimes you snap—or go after him because you can't appear weak.

It may seem like a picnic to the casual observer seeing the big, husky guards sitting around, shooting the breeze at the end of the cellblocks, but it isn't when a whistle blows an emergency: a fight, a riot, a knifing, an escape. So more than a few jailers are like the jailed: tough, sensate types who respect toughness above all else. The kind that like to shove an offensive lineman, break through, and body-slam the quarterback to the turf. Except he is sitting up there in the catwalk in his metal vest, a rifle in his lap, his finger feathering the trigger with constant tension.

Some time later, I interview a pleasant-faced, olive-skin mainliner squatting on a pier under the shed in the upper yard. He's on a classroom break. He says his name is Ali. I hear *Ollie* and assume he's of Italian descent. He's Muslim. We kid about it. I ask him about the guards: "Are a lot of them evil?"

"No," he says. "They're not bad guys. They're just doing their job."

Often a prisoner's judgment is colored by how much time he's doing, how soon he's getting out. Ali should be out in a couple of years.

Historically, prisoners have hated their guards. As a rule, it's the nature of their relationship, because each man has to maintain his self-esteem. A tough, curly blonde lifer told me one day that he had decided to give up his tough-lipped ways and be more Christ-like. He decided to say "good evening" to a certain officer. The officer, who had known him for years, passed him by "as if I were the scum of the earth. I wasn't even worth a look, in his eyes." That's been my experience, too.

DOING TIME

When I walk by, some guards act as if I'm not even there. Not all the guards are like that, of course, but enough are to make you feel a chill.

The strained relationship that sometimes develops between the guards and the inmates is captured in an incident a year ago. A guard went down, fell on the tier. Two mainliners in blue denims went to his aid; mainliners who work and have freedom of movement are not considered high risks. A couple of guards rushed up, misinterpreted what they saw, and started clubbing the inmates trying to help. The two mainliners ended up with concussions and broken arms from the beatings. There are no "good Sams"—good Samaritans—at the Q anymore. Incidents like this deepen the negativity.

If you have any problems with authority—and I myself have a few—you become terribly conscious of the guards. Every time you get a rude reaction or a stony silence, you tighten inside. But after many months, I come to understand that it's what they've been taught: *Don't get close. Over-familiarization is dangerous.* They are indoctrinated though lectures and videos: *You can never trust a con.* As a general policy, especially for those working with the toughest prisoners, this attitude is actually pretty useful. Once a guard gets close, gets too friendly, he or she (there are a few women guards) may do a favor for a con. Then they're compromised. They can be blackmailed for having done the favor, and there's no end to it. But I'm not a con. And prisoner ranks are sprinkled with some pretty decent guys. For the most part, the Q is a Level I and Level II prison—low and medium security prisoners. Still...

One day Father Jack O'Neill, the legendary Catholic chaplain at the Q for eighteen years, returns to the Q. He comes to give a tour of the prison for some relatives and a half-dozen Coast Guard officers. O'Neill is a captain in the Navy Reserve. At his request, I accompany them.

Jack, as he is called by many, leads the quarter-mile trot from the East Gate to the sally port, gesturing and pointing out things and talking in his excited baritone like an Italian tour guide—except Jack is funnier, full of stories and incidents and one-liners. By his girth, you can tell he loves food, especially Italian, and there's something about his joyous spirit and relentless energy that's infectious.

We reach the sally port, the final checkpoint before the cellblocks. Jack stops, hunches over slightly like an umpire behind the plate, points his hairy finger at Ernie the guard and with a face-splitting grin and twinkling Irish eyes, says: "Do I know this man? Do I know this man?" He laughs a throaty laugh, half-hugs Ernie, and the guard becomes someone I've never seen. Ernie is a shy, handsome Black man, invariably polite but emotionless when he checks your brown card or driver's license. But suddenly Ernie is talking and laughing, remembering the good old times with Father O'Neill "smuggling" leftover pasta, canapés, and wedding cake to the prisoners along with some for the guards.

As the first iron gate clangs open, another huge, good-looking, red-mustachioed guard comes through the crowded sally port. Jack again points his hairy finger and cries out, "Tom." Officer Tom lights up, waves wildly, and can't get to shake Jack's hand fast enough. Half over his shoulder and half to Officer Tom, Jack shouts in the shuffling din, "I baptized this guy and married him." Up to this point, I wasn't sure whether the guards could smile. It was amazing to see the difference that twenty years of familiarity, trust, and boisterous good humor could make.

DOING TIME

The graying deputy warden joins our group as host, obviously delighted to do so—anything for Father Jack O'Neill. For the next two hours, we are constantly interrupted by shouts and cheers from the cellblocks: Father Jack, Father O'Neill—or by mainliners in the yard or smiling guards at the 4-post or the Mac Shack checkpoints—guards who never laugh or smile at me. But Jack has them coming alive out of monotonous duty—laughing and smiling. He was the pope of the Q—not just for Catholics but everybody. In the months ahead whenever I mention his name every Black Baptist lifer I meet lights up—and countless others of different stripes.

Even now, Jack spends an hour or two a day from his parish in Point Reyes writing anyone he knows in the hole. If he takes a trip or goes overseas with the reserves, he sends funny postcards to the guys. He is revered in the Black community. One day I was talking to Earl Smith, the Protestant chaplain, about Jack smuggling food into the prison for the guys. Smith said, "Smuggling? The guards helped him carry it in." I mention this to Jack. He says, "Whenever I brought food in, I made sure it was shared equally between the Protestant and Catholic chapels: one third Blacks, one-third whites, one-third Latinos."

The ebullient Jack and the shy McManus, co-chaplains for many years, couldn't be more different, but both contributed greatly in their own way. From McManus I learn wisdom and spiritual depth and I learn to love the prisoners. From Jack I learn to love the guards as well: to see Christ in them as I do the prisoners. They are human beings and they have lives too.

12

SAVED BY THE BLOOD OF JESUS

West Block is one of the largest housing units for prisoners and it's still not big enough. I can see a hundred double-decker, rusty-springed beds running along the length of the ground floor facing five-tiered cellblocks. A con in an orange jumpsuit sits on the edge of one of the beds, smoking a cigarette to the nub. Another is flat out on top of his bunk reading a tattered paperback. A third stares into the gray light oozing through the grimy windows tiers above. All these adult men on "Broadway," as it's called, have only two toilets (converted cells) and nothing to do but time. I aim to bring some sunshine into this terrible, depressing place this morning.

A gaunt face stares out at me through the shaggy hair that wreathes it and the black iron bars that frame it. He has that tired, roadkill look that tells me he's been here more than a couple of times. As it turns out, this is his seventh incarceration. He's nervous and antsy, a little desperate. He just arrived so maybe he's still feeling the sensation of spiders up and down his veins as he goes cold turkey from drugs. I ask him his name, where he's from, what kind of work he does, his drug of choice. Willie's is heroin and, like crack, it is especially tough to shake.

"Tried rehab?"

"I've been saved by the Blood of Jesus," he declares.

"But this is your seventh time here, Willie." I suck in a noisy breath of prison air, eye *him* eyeing *me* uneasily. "Without rehab—."

"The Blood of Jesus is enough."

DOING TIME

"It hasn't worked so far. I think Jesus would like you to go to rehab."

He shakes off the suggestion. He tried rehab, but I'm sure he hadn't really given up the Big H from his heart, then or now. So he's laying it all on Jesus: simple answer to a compound problem. Willie's desperate clinging to the "Blood of Jesus" is Fundamentalism in its naked state.

Later, I have the following exchange with an Hispanic con in Donner. He says:

"*Estoy Cristiano.*"

"What were you raised in?"

"*Catolico.*" Then a thoughtful pause. "What's the difference between Catholic and Christian?"

The poorest-of-the-poor Latinos live on the fringes of society and the fringes of the church. The language baffles them, makes them shy and withdrawn. They lack the clothes or the knowledge of the faith to be comfortable going into a big, concrete church. They do menial work if they can find it and live lives without structures, live day to day. The future is just a word. Along comes hope: *Saved by the Blood of Jesus.* It's something they can cling to—but sometimes not long enough to stay out of the Q.

There are some wonderful Christians in the Protestant chapel working hard at goodness—just like the men at the Catholic chapel. And I'm intrigued by those involved in Fundamentalism, one of the most controversial movements of our day. So, I have a need to check it out further. I look up Fernando, a Latino Christian from New York City and a sometimes jailhouse-minister. He was once a Catholic who, when first incarcerated, would taunt me about Mary and the pope. He's back the second or third time now on a violation. So a touch more humble. He's a decent sort, pudgy and loquacious, with an above-average intelligence and an easy smile on good days. I approach him on the second tier of Donner; he smiles broadly and starts chattering away through the bars. Through our brief, intermittent encounters we have become almost buddies: he acts as though we are co-religionists, and if you believe in "the priesthood of all believers" as so many Christian denominations do, including some fundamentalists—then we are. I tell him I would like to understand him better.

"I believe I've been saved by the Blood of Jesus," Fernando tells me with conviction. "No matter what I do in the future, I'm saved." He almost trembles as he says it, so mind-blowing is this truth to him.

"No matter what you do?"

"No matter what I do."

When you have an addiction, a guarantee can be pretty comforting. I like Fernando and respect his sincerity. He's a good guy with a good heart, honestly struggling with his demons. In my theological world, however, there is a God who loves me madly, but there are no guarantees I will love him so in return. And my love is shown by my actions.

Fernando's Evangelical religion, which permeates so much of the Q, drives me back to its American source: Jonathan Edwards, the great puritan theologian. Like Calvin, Edwards saw man as a "sinner in the hands of an angry God" and believed salvation comes from God alone: Our good works are of no value. Faith alone saves. But he also believed true conversion is evidenced by our good works, not by our feelings.

Now skip forward to late-nineteenth-century America, when William Jennings Bryan, arguing in the Scopes trial for creationism over evolution, said: "The only thing that can save the Bible is *literalism.*" Literalism led to *physicality* as "blood atonement" and "saved by the Blood of Jesus." And sometimes the blood feels more important than the Son's love for the Father in shedding it. A little bit like Mel Gibson's *The Passion.* But Fundamentalists encounter God and lead good lives, and I always encourage them—though our theologies differ.

13

BUCKLE UP BACK TO PRISON

"What are you in for?" I ask through the bars of an Alpine cage, talking to a portly man with a silver buzz on his scalp.

"Violation," he answers, as if he's used to saying it, but resentfully.

"Dirty test?" Parolees are subject to a weekly or monthly test to see if there are drugs in their urine. "Yes."

That yes means he is an addict who has visited the Q multiple times. And the likelihood that his stay of 90, 120, or 180 days will do anything more than provide him a drying-out period is remote. In fact, it is almost certain he will be back here again sooner rather than later, without a cure or any real tools to get well—if he lives.

Sam, a mainliner, reminds me one day that fifty-two out of seventy-three homicides in East Oakland are of ex-cons out of San Quentin. In a sense, the parole system helped seal the fate of these men by its failure. Rigid and self-serving, its primary focus is not solving human problems but punishment. *Punishment.*

At the Q 80 percent of the men have a drug or alcohol problem. A large percent are released within two to three years at most. A large percent return, because of behavior caused by their addiction. So we have a revolving door policy of prison to parole to prison again and again.

The absurdity of the system is especially obvious when drugs and alcohol are *not* involved.

"What are you in for?"

"They got me on a violation."

"Dirty test?"

"Nothing like that."

I'm talking in the yard with a light-skinned Latino. He is intensely sincere. He looks like a together guy, one of those few who's out of place here.

"How long you got to go?"

"Nine months."

It seems like a long time for a violation and he's not your average con. I press on curiously: "What for?"

"I'm driving along minding my business when a police officer stops me because my wife isn't wearing a seatbelt. As the driver, I'm responsible. It's a felony and it violates my parole."

The guy has a wife and kids at home who need him. And my judgment is he's been trying his best. He seems upset, of course, but not as bitter as he might have been. *Nine months in prison for a seatbelt.*

I move to West Block and encounter two men. It's February but the cells are breathlessly hot in the upper tiers and some men, like the two I'm staring at, are down to their shorts. They may have done drugs at some time like millions of other people, but they don't strike me as addicts. There's an adult impatience about the one gripping the bars, talking to me. I picture him as a general contractor when he is "disbarred."

DOING TIME

"You imagine this? Grown men wasting the best years of our lives in cages."

"What happened?" I get the sense it might be unusual.

The man is steaming with indignation. "Broke parole. They said I broke parole."

"How's that?"

Hanging onto the bars, he shakes his head, his big brown eyes on fire, as if I'm not going to believe what he's going to tell me.

"I watch my son's Little League game. After, I let him off at his mom's, but he leaves his bat and glove on the back seat of the car. I'm drivin' home in my old Ford, thinkin' about it, when the *po*-lice pull me over. I ain't been drinkin,' I ain't doin' no drugs. I stopped that long time a go. They find I'm on parole, they send me back to jail for a year for violatin' parole."

"What was the charge?"

"Possession of a deadly weapon: my son's baseball bat!"

If this sounds incredible, you must understand that, depending on the conditions of parole, a man can be tossed back into prison for nine months of his life if he is caught in a house with an open can of beer—even if he himself hasn't touched a drop. How likely is it that a man on parole is never going to be in a house of his family or friends without an open beer-can for, say, three years? This would be unlikely for any person in any social class, but the poor especially live on beer. It is self-medication against being at the bottom of a capitalist society. For the most part, they lack the opportunities to transcend their neighborhoods or their addictions. They can't go to the Betty Ford Clinic—only movie stars and millionaires can.

The most the Q is designed to do—and at a very high expense—is to dry them out. No in-prison rehab. No real in-house connection to recovery groups. But drying out only takes one month, not three, four, or nine. To toss these addicted men—who usually lack a key ingredient for getting their act together—into prison without a realistic program for rehabilitation is punitive, cruel, and useless.

Imagine you are one of them, like this middle-aged bedraggled con sleeping in the cell in front of me. Sunspots dot his pale forehead above his veiny nose, and he looks undernourished. Your parole officer has released you in San Francisco the same place where you were picked up. Those are the rules. You are not allowed to live with your sister, a nurse, a half hour away in San Mateo, because it is outside San Francisco County. You say the only chance you have to stay out of prison is with your sister in a new scene. You have begged for this a number of times but the system says no. You end up in the booze-soaked, drug-ridden Tenderloin district of San Francisco. You have no job, so you are living on the streets trying to stay sober and to stay out of jail, slipping into door-ways and alleys whenever you spot a cop or a cruiser. Then it happens.

"I was in the Tenderloin making my way toward Saint Anthony's when a parole officer dragged me in. I wasn't doing anything bad. I wasn't dirty. I wasn't out of the Q twenty-four hours and I got caught up in a sweep. Why? Because I wasn't supposed to be in the Tenderloin."

A prisoner can't go back to his old place, where he committed his crime, but can't go to a new place farther away either.

The system is a *gotcha*.

One inmate said to me, "If you were arrested in hell, that's where they'd parole you."

Then there's the poor guy in Donner who is back in prison for a year on a violation. Attempted robbery, dealing drugs, beating his wife? No. Doing 85 miles per hour in a 65 mile per hour zone. But that's the system's motto: *punishment, not rehabilitation.*

This first year or so that I'm working with the men in the cellblocks, I hear over and over again: "I wasn't doing drugs, didn't take a drink, and I'm back in again for another five months." I know many parolees lie and deceive themselves. When they say, "All I did was miss my weekly appointment with my parole officer," they don't also say "because I would have given him a dirty test." Or when the bald-headed con who complained to me one day about a nine-month stint at the Q: "All I was doing was urinating against the wall." He didn't mention it was near a school and he had a well-earned reputation in his neighborhood for being "the mad flasher."

There are good parole officers who care about the men on their lists and work to help them using "tough love." But too many are hardened by the system, just as much as some prisoners can be.

One night I call Jerry, an ex-priest and former classmate of mine in the seminary. He has held, like a number of expriests, a major position in both state and federal parole departments. He is a compassionate man, but he is also a lawyer. He is no soft touch after thirty-plus years of dealing with nasty, lazy, or cunning cons. He has seen their spitting viciousness and subhuman behavior and has had his good heart broken by more than a few. He's also seen the other side—parole officers who are in it just for the money, and who do only what they have to do.

Jerry works long days into the night and weekends, too. He sees the young men who come before him not as losers, as some do, but as redeemable. The irony is that when he was a young priest, a thief kept breaking into the poor box in his parish. It bugged Jerry so he kept his eye peeled. Then one day he caught the thief in the act and, cassock flying, chased him down. It made the papers all over the country: *Priest makes flying tackle on poor-box thief.* My classmates and I kidded him mercilessly. "Jesus wouldn't have tackled him, Jerry. He would have given him the second collection." So, you couldn't call Jerry soft on crime.

Just when I think I've seen the worst of what the system can do, I run into a beautiful Black man in Alpine one day. The weak light of his cell makes his sweat-beaded ebony scalp shine. It's hot on the fifth tier and the air dense and musty with the odors of five-hundred men in small cages. He has this look that you see on the faces of so many prisoners. It's a resigned look that seems to say: *I've been down so long it feels like up to me.* We talk. He tells me they gave him a year for breaking parole. He has a family out there so they're suffering without him, but he doesn't mention that. People don't realize that when you sentence a man, you sentence his family as well.

"A year is pretty heavy duty," I say. "What did you do?"

"I was falsely accused of a crime." It happens a lot with felons and parolees; they're the "usual suspects."

"But you were cleared?"

"Don't matter. The judge threw out the charges, but my parole officer said I was on parole. Shouldn't have been around there."

My stomach knots up with anger once more. What kind of system snatches a man from his family and throws him back in prison for a false charge? I shake my head, take hold of his strong, coal-black hands through the bars, and ask him if there's anybody he would like to pray for. He mentions his family, of course, then he adds:

"And the homeless folks on the streets."

I choke up. Only the poor think instinctively of those worse off than themselves. It's one of those moments when I am deeply touched and reminded how much more I get from the men at the Q than I give.

14
LETTING GO OF ANGER

Love makes the world go round but anger makes the Q tick. It lurks just beneath the surface like an alligator in a swamp, prowling for an insult or perceived offense or violation of the rules—prisoner rules. It's behind the curtness and tension of the guards. That one-down feeling. Serious crime and drugs come from angry men who too often come from angry parents. The attorney general of California says over 900,000 children in a given year, from infants to five-year-olds, are exposed to domestic violence. Almost 200,000 calls a year are received by law enforcement. Most of these involve guns or other weapons. These highly malleable children start school with attention deficit disorder and aggressive behavior, unconsciously desperate to let it out. At the earliest age they have absorbed like language their world of danger and fear. All this leads to poor grades, low self-esteem, a sense of failure, and a need to lash out at somebody. The Q is full of men like this.

One day at the Catholic chapel I ask McManus about a certain model prisoner. The man is a lifer but he's bright, responsible, and greatly respected by his peers, and he's also initiating good things.

"You think he might be paroled?" I ask.

McManus, who likes the man, shakes his head. "He's not ready yet. He hasn't dealt with his anger."

I can see it as soon as he says it. The crime that earned him life came out of some kind of rage. He has an edge. He's not quite at peace after all the years. There's often a tension about him like a prizefighter just before he enters the ring. And there's plenty more like him but much less intelligent. Physical and chiseled, they've gone through life like a series of explosions. They tend to cope with their problems using their bodies. And while some are learning new tricks, it takes time.

Shortly after, I run into a powerful-looking, shaven-headed, bare-chested prisoner in Alpine exercising vigorously in his tiny cell. His cellie is snoozing in the upper bunk. He's a mixture of white, Indian, and something else. He tells me he's in for the tenth time.

"Tenth?" I say.

"Yeah."

"Drugs and alcohol?"

"Nope. Beat up my girlfriend."

"Were you drunk?"

"Nope. Angry. She pushes my buttons. And she really, really knows how to do it."

"Tried anger management?"

"Ten times."

"Why didn't it work?"

"I wasn't ready for it. I was hoping the course would do it *for* me. I'm ready now." He keeps pressing his palms isometrically into his dull cream wall. Every time he takes a deep breath I get a sense of what a powerful explosion he would make if triggered.

This prisoner makes me realize, for the first time almost, something I should have guessed early on. Drugs and alcohol are not the root causes of crime—anger is. Anger at being one down, a fringe player in society, a loser, a dropout, a failure. Drugs and alcohol are nothing but self-medication for these men but it can relax their limited self-control with violent results.

I keep running into anger in the cellblocks. I'm alert to it now. I ask a ruggedly handsome Burt Reynolds look-alike why he hasn't contacted his father in five years. He gives me a cool, silent look. Then he says, "The last time I saw my father he had a gun to my head."

Anger can be genetic. A family tradition.

The lockdowns that happen almost monthly and the "controlled movement"—Hispanics or Blacks go to chow separately, for example—are usually caused by a fight or knifing brought on by a remark or a slight, real or imagined. And the gangs of Norteños, Sureños, Crips, Bloods, and Skinheads that gather and stealthily maraud on the tiers or in the yards are nothing but communities of anger and fear: joint protection against the slights or threats of others. They squeeze new cons to do favors, then squeeze them to pay them back.

I imagine a gang leader to have his chin out like a little Jimmy Cagney begging for a fight. But one day a repeat offender points out to me the guy who calls the shots in Donner. He is not awesomely physical; in fact, he looks shriveled and grizzled to me. But he's smart and knows cell life, so he calls the shots for his "runners." But his counterpart for the Crips is as bristling tough as the hardest hitting NFL cornerback you've ever seen.

Alice Roosevelt said Bobby Kennedy reminded her of an angry young priest. I can identify with that. After training to be a priest for six years and more of obedience and silent subjugation, I came out on fire to change the world but ran into a reactionary cardinal who wanted to keep things exactly the way they were. He believed there was no problem that could not be solved by a new building. Not new ideas or movements. New York Irish, he believed he had dealt with the race problem in Watts when he said, "We put up a new high school for *them.*"

You can imagine the anger this would stir in young, idealistic priests. But the real anger for me comes from inside. Like many young priests, I never realized that my anger was not caused by the cardinal so much as by my own spirit of independence and my own internal fight against celibacy. With God's help I thought I could live the obedience and the celibate life. I wanted very much to do so for the love of Christ and for many years I did. But it was as if I had a fire within me that couldn't be banked. No amount of prayer seemed sufficient to put it out.

I left the priesthood in anger. It was an anger different from a prisoner's, but I can empathize. I have known the impulse to lash out, then the seizure-like effects that left me empty and loveless. It took me some time in therapy to understand its source: My contempt for authoritarian authorities. My flesh burning with anger. My ego crying out for fairness from a cardinal who held "liberal" young priests under suspicion. His own priests were the enemy. But anger is anger, so I can empathize with a con's.

One early afternoon, my stomach rumbling, my neck achy from looking over, around, and through countless cell bars at caged inmates, I catch up with Deacon George heading back to the chapel. I tell him what's on my mind lately. He responds. "I stomped out of the confessional and the church, started drinking myself unconscious for twenty-five years."

"But I've heard you say you drank because you felt lousy about yourself."

"Yeah, and that was the main reason. I was angry at God and the world because I didn't like who I was or how I felt about myself. *Why me, God?* It took me fifteen years in therapy to find it out."

"That's a long time."

We pass by the impassive stares of the guards at the post and a handful of mainliners in blue taking a break from work or class. Anger management class perhaps.

"As much as 80 to 90 percent of the prisoners have deep-seated anger inside themselves they've never dealt with and it's just waiting to be triggered," he says. "Until they honestly go through therapy and come to grips with it, they can't change their lives and move on."

I ask him about the prisoner McManus said wasn't ready.

"He's a really good guy with a solid spiritual base but," Deacon George pauses, shakes his head sadly, "at least two people have tried to get him to face his anger in therapy but he brushed them off."

"He's a really good guy. Too bad."

"Anger management classes are useful but they don't get at the underlying stuff." He squeezes his fist tight against his belly.

Deacon George can be impatient and brusque at times but he's generous to a fault, his heart beats for every man in the Q, and he is rarely angry now. Then again, he's seventy-two. I can imagine how this fiery, spirit-driven man must have seethed at times when younger. But he was a therapist and drug counselor and he put himself through a psychiatric "MRI" weekly for fifteen years so he knows what he's talking about. I learn a lot of things from George. He's street-smart, "belly smart."

My thoughts about anger the next few weeks inspire a homily on the subject one Sunday. I start it off with a movie as I often do. Cons love movies and comic books.

I tell them I rented a video of *The Sopranos,* the hottest show on HBO TV. It's about a small-time Mafia boss, Tony, who sends his soldier into a house of prostitution whose owner has been "skimming." The soldier whacks two or three people in the head with a lead pipe, then kneecaps the owner as he pleads for mercy. Tony smiles with satisfaction at his soldier's "good work."

Then Tony is telling his rather attractive psychiatrist about his anxiety attacks. She suggests the attacks might be connected with his anger, which is hair-trigger quick. He is a tough guy who can show no mercy.

Like Tony, I tell them, lots of guys at the Q come out of angry homes. What makes them angry? The absence of love, the feeling of injustice, the feeling of being one down, not worth much. "I won't take stuff from nobody." It's understandable. But until you let go of the anger and make room for mercy and forgiveness, you can't heal.

And when someone from "the outside" says, "I forgive but I can't forget, he killed my daughter, and now I can't wait to see him squirm and burn in the electric chair"—that person is deader spiritually than the man in the chair.

This reminds me of the follow-up to Dominic's story. I catch him one day covered with sweat in the lower yard where he's just finished playing handball. He's a good player. Muscled hands, big rolling shoulders. We chat for a while. He's at peace. I ask him again how he feels about the snitch who lied about his role in the kidnapping. The man who got him life at the Q instead of seven years.

"I was real angry for a while. I mean *real* angry. Angry enough to kill. But I found I wasn't happy—hating. Then I ran into Father O'Neill and Father McManus. They taught me about love. And George. I'd never heard the word *love* before. I was a pretty tough Portagee, you know. Started coming to chapel. God was just a word, but I was looking for something. Little by little I let go of the anger. Forgave the guy."

I don't say anything. I just let him talk. When they get to know and trust you, they like to tell their story more than once. There's not many they can tell it to.

"Funny isn't it?" Dominic says, dabbing some stray sweat on his hairy arm. "When I let go of the anger, God took its place.

"But something else. One day—I'm about five years here—I spot the snitch who lied. I couldn't believe it. He finally made it. He sees me across the yard and his face turns white. I mean *dead white* like the blood drained out. I walk over to him and I can tell he was *scared.* He was sure he was a dead man sooner or later. We're two feet apart. I'm looking at him, he's looking at me. Then I said, 'I forgive you.' I meant it. It was hard but I meant it. He didn't know what to make of it. He didn't say a word but all the guys were watching. I just walked away."

I wonder to myself if *I* could have done that after twenty years in prison.

"If you want some peace in your life, you've got to let go of anger. Then God'll come."

I walk away from the earthy Dominic thinking maybe I've been talking to a saint. He forgave the guy from the heart. They weren't just words he was saying. He forgave the guy who had stolen his family, his friends, his fiancée, and a good chunk of his life.

There is no puff or fluff in a prison. It's a bare-bones reality and often very ugly, but there are moments—like this one—when the most beautiful things come to light.

15

"THE GANG OF TEN"

It's a Wednesday evening, April 2002. The days are getting longer. I stop to watch a flaming sun sink gorgeously into the Bay waters, then I'm inside the Q once more. Now I'm sitting in a circle of folding chairs in the chapel sanctuary, along with Father Peter Togñi and ten lifers. It's the only space available besides McManus's cramped, book-lined office. I know most of the men from Sundays in the choir and on the altar, though not as well as I will get to know them over the next two years. They are surely diverse: four Latinos, two Anglos, two African Americans, one Vietnamese, and one Filipino. The group will change some as men are transferred or released. I've been inside the belly of the beast for six years and touched its heart at times, and now I will go deeper into its soul.

Phil, a devout lifer who on Sundays looks like Tony of *The Sopranos* in a cassock, got wind of Archbishop Levada's pastoral leadership program for educating the laity of San Francisco in theology and scripture. So Phil wrote the archbishop: Why not at the Q too? *Voila!* Togñi, who fills in at Sunday Mass sometimes and in summers, volunteered. After a couple of years he asks me to join him.

DOING TIME

Togñi is a progressive Jesuit theologian. He wears glasses and has increasingly fewer strands of sandy hair on his head. He has a friendly, unassuming style that easily sees the comic side of life—and he squints whimsically at human conundrums. Like many Jesuits, his background is not ordinary. He grew up in a Swiss-Italian farming family in King City, is a Yale man (though I found out by accident), and is now assistant academic dean at the University of San Francisco.

Togñi lets the men teach themselves. It is a nice model. Each week the men are given an assignment in pairs to come up with five questions to ask the group regarding the weekly material. We are covering part of the blue, glossy-covered paperback *The Catechism of the Catholic Church*—specifically, conscience and the natural law. I explain that much of the natural law can be known by reason; for example, you should not kill, and so on. But the totality of the natural law, and the "law in our hearts" are often gray and unclear. Most of the men are tough guys with hard pasts, some *really* hard. Invariably, theological reflection and insights lead to humble and penitent disclosures: "I was a *rotten* kid. I mean *rotten*." And, "I was a skirt-chaser. All I cared about was myself." There is no other place in the prison where a man can show weakness, and it is this sharing of vulnerabilities that binds them in community and, yes, in love. Fear may make the Q go round, but here in the chapel it's love.

One night Joni, the administrator of the pastoral leadership program, brings a writer for the *San Francisco Catholic* and some lay people to observe the group. It is amazing how little people on the outside know of what goes on inside prison. *Prison* is a word like *Siberia*. The prisoners who form the circle with them are so bright, so human, so funny, so patient with their terrible lot in life, that the visitors can hardly com-

79

prehend it when Trace, the blunt-talking country-western type says: "Almost everyone here has murdered someone, ya know?" Not quite but almost. But these men have been caged ten, twenty, thirty years. They are not the same men who entered way back when. As the weeks pass, I am touched by the love these men have for each other. In this awful place, midst threats and violence from prisoners and the cold contempt of guards, struggling with rage then bitterness at their fate—life in prison—these men have discovered love. It was not something they knew growing up in poverty, violence, reform school. They knew only toughness, anger, and revenge: the keys to survival on the streets. They were life's collateral damage. But this particular evening, Trace, a white man, and Oscar, a Black, two of the ruggedest, most fearsome guys you want to meet, are sharing with the group what the men in the circle mean to them.

"I came to know about God loving me through you guys," Trace says, making the circle with his eyes. "That's the truth. That's real. I couldn't spell the word before this." He hunches over, his fingers laced between his knees. He nods his head toward Oscar, a couple of seats to his right. "And that guy— he's the one got me interested in the chapel and, you know, God. If it weren't for him…"

"I didn't do nothing," Oscar protests with a grin. "It's all God's work. And I was just as bad as you before I got involved with these guys."

"All I know was God was using *you*," Trace points at Oscar.

They grin shyly. White and Black, they are buddies. Their trust in each other is as solid as their biceps.

Trace, up for parole next month, starts worrying out loud about it. "Without the love and support of you guys, I may not make it on the outside." He anxiously rubs the dark tattoo on the back of his hand. The chances of his being released are low at best. Hope in prison is only a mirage. "I don't think church people on the outside will ever accept me. And once they find I've been in prison so long, what chance will I have?"

"You'll do just fine, Trace," says Joe, a balding, articulate Latino with a broad smile. "Just fine." The rest of us chime in with our support.

"You've got a beautiful heart, man," Oscar adds.

And I'm thinking he's real and honest and straight as any man I've ever met. No facades, no false fronts: They were all burned away when he was going through hell. And though he's still in hell, it's only his body, and it sounds strange because outside the chapel prisoners never talk like this.

It's May now and another Wednesday evening. I name the group "the gang of ten." They all laugh. We are on the subject of grace—the divine indwelling through the grace of baptism and the sacraments. A couple of the men *ooh* and *ahh*, revel in the beauty of the notion that God dwells in us. *Honest.* One reads aloud with feeling the famous line from Augustine: "God became man that men might become Gods." These cons are not "born agains," though they have beautiful experiences, too. There's a warm glow but no emotional arm waving. Catholic grace is more often a quiet, interior, gradual thing. It may be hard to understand how killers and men guilty of other very serious crimes can reach such a point of tenderness in their rediscovered faith. But these men have a great deal of time—quiet, alone time in their prison cells. The reception center is noisy bedlam. The mainline North Block is more low-keyed and subdued. It provides them the opportunity for reflection on their failures, their sins, and their angry, wasted lives—once the anger subsides. The testosterone level lowers and they mellow out once they move into prayer.

Prayer is big among the lifers active in the Catholic chapel, but it's also big among the lifers active in the Protestant chapel, and the Jewish and Muslim centers as well. I see prayer in many others trying to turn their lives around. It brings a peace to the men that shows in their faces. But peace is often preceded by years of anger, bitterness, violence, and drugs, even within the prison.

Like most people of a religious bent, I struggle with prayer, even as a priest. I remember John Thom, a wonderful young priest in graduate school, saying to me, "There are moments when I find prayer terribly *sweet.*" John, the manliest of priests, from a farm in North Dakota, had turned down a $50,000 bonus to sign with the LA Dodgers. I asked this strapping farm boy once about his skill. "Denny," he said shyly with a smile, "I could throw a baseball through a brick wall." And I wondered whether his heroic rejection of a big-league career was what "won" him the gift of prayer from God. As a priest myself, I gave it my best but I didn't always feel completely generous in my gift to God. Pretty girls distracted me and I envied happily married couples. I dwelled on my loneliness too much and maybe that caused my divided heart. I felt wonderful moments in God's presence but too often I felt the desert. After I left the priesthood, prayer became lost in the rush and swirl of becoming a material man and of making a living.

Still I desired God. Maybe he was always in the back of my head like a gently nagging mother. Then one night, long out of the corporate rat race, after a day of consulting in the Silicon Valley, I ran across *The Cloud of Unknowing* at a bookstore in Menlo Park. It's a spiritual classic by an anonymous fourteenth-century Cistercian monk. I had heard of the book but never read it. Such a catchy title.

Simply but beautifully, the English monk urges the reader to leave all created things behind in "the cloud of forgetting" and enter "the cloud of unknowing" through a prayer that is a simple reaching out to God in a single word. This mantra-like word, which the reader chooses—*God, love,* or so on—keeps the distractions at bay while one longs simply for God, he says. Easier said than done. But doable, I find.

I started haltingly at first, twenty minutes a day—and not every day. It was a discipline from a sense of duty and my old friend guilt as much as a desire for God. Only gradually has it become difficult for me to miss a day of this prayer of longing. I often start with the opening of Psalm 42: "As the doe longs for running streams, so my soul longs for you, O, God." Sometimes I have more distractions than sand fleas on the beach. My lifestyle is so often out of sync with the mystical, yet I can't give this prayer up, for it bequeaths small, tender moments in which I can "taste" God's presence. I feel it is my one toehold on eternity.

A couple of years ago, Father Thomas Keating, a famous Trappist monk, visited the Q. I remember the spring day vividly: A tall, aging ascetic in a belted white habit, his big bony arms and hands gesturing at twenty men sitting in a circle around him. The men, Catholic and Protestant, attentive to every soft-spoken word. His message, like his several books, was about his mission to spread the word that contemplation and the mystical life is not just for monks but for everyone. Maybe the most powerful part of his message was his own gentle spirit and peaceful demeanor.

Then he led us in "centering prayer." After a period of silence, he gave instructions to the mainliners, and a couple nuns who were present, to "put everything out of your mind and repeat to yourself that one syllable word you've chosen—*God, love*—whenever a distraction pops into your mind. Focus on God's presence inside you. Love him there." For twenty minutes or so the sanctuary was in perfect silence. At the end, he asked for the men to comment on their experience. All were astonished at how quickly the time had passed. "I couldn't believe it when you said the twenty minutes was up," one Protestant mainliner said.

The centering-prayer sessions continue weekly every Monday night to this day. Many of those men in the first session are still in the group. And many continue the practice of this prayer in their cells. In fact, over the years I have passed out dozens of *Locked Up and Free* pamphlets, in English and Spanish, explaining this very ecumenical approach to God. Would you believe—contemplative monks in the Q?

16
A DRUGGIE AND JFK

The gang of ten leaves me with a kind of glow, the feeling that I am providing a bit of solace and stoking their hope. There are plenty of others of all faiths, and none at all, struggling to find their way. They are the good guys, but they are not the only ones here. I must keep reminding myself that they are but a small slice of the Q pie—especially when I see a very young prisoner in shackles being escorted to his cell by a burly guard. The men in the yard stop and eye him, sizing him up like birds of prey. You can see the barely concealed fright in the young man's eyes as he passes.

As I make my way to West Block and Donner, I remember a conversation with a veteran con. A young Filipino prisoner was in Novato, thirty minutes away, in the "prison wing hospital." The young man was in very bad shape with a perforated rectum. I asked the veteran how it happened.

"A broom handle. He was too terrified to report it to the guards or squeal on the guys who did it."

"When did they find out?"

"After he spent three or four days in agony on his cot without eating, his cellie reported it to the guards. Now the guy is badly infected."

"That's a shame." I shake my head. "Happen often?" I ask McManus and Deacon George, curious as to whether the rumors are true. McManus says, "How and where would they do it?" And he's anything but naïve.

Deacon George, has seen everything in twenty-five years. He says, "You bring a young prisoner into a crowd of older, hardened criminals, and he's going to be abused sexually and other ways."

"Don't the guards keep them from—."

"There's five-hundred men in the cellblock. You can't watch them every minute."

Recent law in California that says minors are to be treated as adults if they commit a serious crime has been described as barbaric. It epitomizes the current anti-rehabilitation stance of both the system and the people.

I keep walking on to the West Block and revisit Mateo, a young Portagee from Contra Costa County. I first ran into Mateo while looking for someone else. That often happens, they move people around so much. I honestly can't tell you why I start investing time in a particular man as I troll the tiers. A look in his eye. Some mutual joking up front. Neediness. Maybe that's what I saw in Mateo. I think he's slowly starting to listen to my input on drug addiction. I *think*. No one else ever talks to them about it. The system just tosses them in the slammer and hope they get the message. You wouldn't run a business that way *unless* you saw keeping the prison filled with bodies *as* the business.

At first, Mateo plays cool, the tough guy. Then he starts being vulnerable and reveals more about himself.

"The last time they let me out, my dad picked me up."

"And—?"

"He was high on coke but the guard didn't spot it. He fooled him. So, I was high within three hours." Mateo is matter of fact rather than penitent.

"How you doing?"

He shrugs, lying on his cot. Is he apathetic or irreverent? Then he asks, "You want to see a picture of my girl?"

It's almost a flip question and there's a smirk on his face that, intent on building a bridge, I fail to notice.

He stands up and slips what looks like stationery through the bars with a picture of his girl looking straight at me. She's very pretty—and she's totally naked. For a flash I wonder how a girl that striking falls for a guy like Mateo. But he's good-looking, and bars must make a guy harder to get. I give it back to him, shake my head sadly at the insult, and walk away. In prison, you practice tough love and tough religion. It's the only thing they understand. Sometimes.

A month later, he's at my Sunday communion service— he's a Catholic—telling me he heard what I was trying to tell him. Monday I check the computer printouts with the name and location of every prisoner. He's not on it. He's out of the Q.

DOING TIME

A year later, I've almost forgotten about Mateo when I hear him calling my name above the din in West Block. He seems very different, energized as I greet him through the bars, unembarrassed by this new incarceration. He tells me about this wonderful woman who spent hours talking to him about Jesus. She gave him some inspiring books about God. He shows me a stack of attractive, glossy-covered, Funda-mentalist paperbacks and tells me he's a changed man on the way to salvation. I encourage him to stay on the road. And I hope his dad doesn't pick him up at the gate this time.

Every so often I am surprised by a complete misfit: a man, white-faced and clean-cut, innocent-looking as a dove, his head bobbing in a swarm of poor Blacks, Mexicans, and whites with drug-drained cheeks and tattooed bodies. Your instincts say he has no business being there—or does he? Is it more than a bungled defense? Probably.

McManus sends me to check on one of them. The inmate's father, a prominent Boston lawyer and concerned parent, has been pestering McManus almost daily, as if he were a tippable concierge at the Ritz Hotel in Boston.

I spot him on the second tier of Donner. His cell door is unlocked—the men are not settled in yet after breakfast. He has the smooth brush of brown hair and confident good looks of John F. Kennedy. He's almost a look-alike. I nickname him JFK in my mind.

"Where are you from?" I ask.

"Nantucket."

"You know Win Hindle?"

"I dated one of the Hindle girls."

Win Hindle was the number two man at the Digital Equipment Corporation and my boss. Quite a coincidence. Then he tells me he went to the prestigious Portsmouth

Priory—William Buckley's Catholic prep school—tried Stanford Medical School but found it too theoretical, or so he says, and then got into venture capital in the Silicon Valley.

"What got you into prison?"

"Securities violation. I allowed investors who weren't qualified into my venture fund. My girlfriend caught me three-timing her, then hired a detective who followed me around and unearthed the violations." He says this unrepentantly as if his girlfriend committed the crime.

"How much time?"

"Eight years."

It sounds high for that crime.

The next week I see JFK in his cell with the cell door open and prisoners stopping to check with him on this and that: hearings for shorter sentences, parole, release dates, and so on. He looks like he's running for governor, cool and smooth in the midst of a tier full of buzz-headed, tattooed whites, retread (recidivist) Blacks, and put-down browns. He sweeps the tier—a role he has volunteered for *unwisely,* McManus tells me later. The inmate who sweeps the tier is expected to pass notes, packages, and *drugs.* If he refuses to pass meth or weed down the tier, he could be a victim. And if he does pass on the drugs, he's implicated and can end up doing more time.

JFK's eyes are always moving, more urbanely than most shifty-eyed. Maybe it's all the interruptions, guys poking their heads in his cell.

"Eight years is a long time for a securities violation," I tell him. "Michael Miliken got only fifteen minutes, then a teaching post at UCLA School of Business."

"He had a lot more money than I do." JFK gives me a bitter, knowing look packaged in a smile to say that Miliken bought his way out.

I change the subject. "How you doing spiritually?"

"Good," he says, his eyes moving, still on the alert.

But I can tell his mind is still in the fast-buck lane. He's more upset about his rich, embittered fiancée who had his dog and his horses put to sleep. I don't think he really believes he's in prison yet.

Back at the chapel, McManus says JFK's father keeps calling from Boston, seemingly demanding special treatment. McManus says archly, "I will not be some rich man's lackey."

"That con is going to learn the hard way," Deacon George says gruffly. "I warned him about being a tier-sweeper."

I run across JFK the next week. He's no longer the tier sweeper but the clerk for the guards in Donner. He talks smoothly about getting his secretary to send him books. "I'm going crazy with nothing to read." He tells me with half-time—a sentence reduction for good behavior—he'll be out in four years and would like to get an MBA at Stanford quicker than usual. One year max at Stanford instead of two.

"Can you do that?"

"As long as I pay the full tuition," he says jauntily. "They just want the money."

He goes on about the MBA giving him more confidence to operate at Silicon Valley's higher altitudes. Then his winning smile closes down for a moment. He looks quite serious. He says, "I'd like to go to confession."

It strikes me as genuine this time. I pass the request on to McManus.

"I think he's turning around," says Deacon George, who has also visited him.

A couple of weeks later he is transferred to another prison.

17
MORE "GANG OF TEN"

Prison is a world of secrets nobody wants revealed: from the warden, to the guards, to the prisoners—all of them have secrets, just like any of us.

Togñi and I are sitting around in a circle as usual with the gang of ten, keeping a firm grip on our secrets because in our sanctuary circle is Barbara, the archdiocesan psychologist. We have finished the thick Catholic catechism and are moving on to the ministry of consolation. Barbara, an attractive blonde in her fifties, is leading the course, which once again is more like a group process. She is gracious and poised and has her stuff together, though the prison has dressed her in oversized white coveralls this first night because she forgot and wore a blue dress. Blue is a no-no, we remind her. She starts by explaining how important the rites of the grieving process are—wakes, the funeral Mass, the Jewish shivah—in dealing with loss. Perceptively, she sees that some of the gang of ten are still dealing with loss. It turns into a grief session.

Gabriel, a dark, handsome Mexican, speaks softly in heavily accented English, pausing in between the phrases to pick the right word.

"I lost my wife, my son—then my daughter—in twelve months." His eyes fill. He lowers his head. Grown men don't cry, not in prison. "I couldn't go to my wife's funeral unless shackled in chains hand and foot and accompanied by two guards. And I had to go at my own expense. I killed her—my wife. I feel I did. She was healthy and fine before I went to prison. A year later, I could see she was a different woman." He pauses. Takes in a long breath.

Gabriel is a very private, shy person. I am surprised. This is the most I have ever heard him say. It's like he's been waiting for the opportunity.

"I wanted to end my life. My faith was lost—in the past." He pauses again. "But Roberto started spending time with me." Roberto is the gentle Spanish-speaking lay volunteer on Sundays for years now. "He saved my life. That's when I found God."

I sit there in the dimly lit chapel, staring at Gabriel, trying to comprehend what it would be like to suffer such overwhelming loss—while in the steely cold confines of prison.

Trace, triggered by Gabriel, discloses next. He has a purple diamond etched on the back of his hand and a "been through hell and back" face. There's tough, tanned wiriness about him and a set to his mouth that would make you hesitate to pick a fight with him. Then he starts talking.

"I lost my mother—she was an alcoholic—at an early age. I was still pretty young and my father abandoned me. She was my only love." He leans over and stares at the sanctuary floor, his mouth set reflectively as he remembers it all. "If the chaplain isn't there, it's really tough to get bad news. A guard tosses a piece of paper into your cell with the news: *Your mother died.* For a second you consider going to the funeral. But you'd be in chains with burly prison guards on your right and left. It would shame the family. And you can't cry—can't show your feelings in prison—except here in this chapel—can't show weakness. Toughness is everything in prison. The warden is tough, the guards are tough, the prisoners are tough.

"So for a few days you skip meals and jogging in the yard and wallow in your grief until your cellie returns. Prison is a twisted place. A guy gets drunk on pruno [alcohol illegally

made by the prisoners]. Then everybody urges him on to bor-
row a shiv and fix the guy down the tier who done him wrong.
Most guys in North Block live without God. I did for years." He
pauses and looks at Barbara. "You know most of us here killed
somebody." That's always on his mind.

He goes on. It's Trace's night. This is the circle where you
can say things you can't say anywhere else.

"We're not the sharpest tools in the shed here."

He looks at Barbara again. He doesn't want anyone to
think he's anything special or anything he's not. It's a kind of
fear of his but it comes across as a radical hard-bought honesty and makes him a strong and compelling figure. Trace has
been in prison for over twenty years. But he's changed.

"I can't discuss God—the key to my life now—with my
older prison buddies. They wouldn't know what I was talking
about."

God was just a swear word for him once and in a moment
of weakness it still can be. He wasn't blinded by the light or
knocked off a horse. He doesn't sound remotely like a born-
again. His faith is chiseled out of the hard rock of life behind
bars. His Jesus is a gritty one, the one on the cross.

Outside the Q, the warm summer nights are lovely. Pink
sunsets over the still bay waters, a river of fog flowing slowly
over the city in the distance, causing the tourists to shiver.
Normal in this world of microclimates. You can understand
how developers lust to have the Q demolished to make room
for some multimillion-dollar development. But this Wednesday
evening, as we gather in our circle, we know that the Q is still
here, and that we're in it.

Bobby is missing from the group. He is in the hole. How
long? You never know. Two weeks, two months, two years. That's
half the torture. Bobby and a couple of others, egged on by a jail-

house lawyer, were petitioning for certain rights—more courses in Asian and Latino and Black history. Wiser cons tried to discourage them: you have no rights in prison. The guards found some contraband in Bobby's cell, from a recently departed cellie most likely. Some guards can find anything they want in your cell even when it's not there. The sad thing, Bobby was up for a release date. With this incident he may never get out.

Midsummer, mid-July, is the last session of grief counseling. In trios, Barbara, the psychologist, has us share obituaries and first feelings about death. Tito, a short, broad-shouldered Filipino, normally ebullient, recalls with some emotion entering the Q for the first time. You can see him tighten with the memory of his feelings. Fifteen years ago.

"These big, muscular guys, tattoos all over their bodies, leered at me as I passed. I was young and small, my body undeveloped then, and I was scared. Then, I was only two months behind bars when I was falsely accused of trying to kill another inmate."

An anonymous accusation, often in a note, is taken with the utmost gravity in prison. Any accusation, however slimy the source, is presumed to be true. It would never hold up in court but it does in prison.

"I was thrown into the hole for two weeks. Then the adjustment center for two years."

I shake my head. The adjustment center is another version of solitary. Then Tito adds ironically:

"Solitary confinement saved my life."

He doesn't say how, but I have a hunch he was isolated, "protected" from being raped and abused, and he had two years to think about his life. But sometimes people go insane there.

For Tito, prison was his first encounter with death.

Just before the session closes, the psychologist asks a probing question:

"At what age would you prefer to die?"

The group mulls the question for a while. It makes you think of something you don't like to think about. We secretly feel we are never going to die. Inimitable Trace scratches his head, then in his down-home style lightens the night.

"I don't want to get *real* old. I mean when a guy isn't able to wipe his own rear anymore, it doesn't make much sense to go on."

The gang breaks up.

It's late August. Bobby has been in the hole for over a month now. All of us are depleted by his absence. He has been inside the Q since he was a kid and there's always the biggest toothiest smile on his Malayan face. He's a convert and a "spiritual," as the prisoners say: one who has turned his life and imprisonment over to God. He has been active for years in the Squires, a bunch of cons who meet with groups of troubled adolescents to get them to straighten out their lives and keep out of "this terrible place."

A week prior, Bobby smuggles a note out to the gang of ten through a buddy. "I am present with all of you in spirit and I am reading along with you. My spirits are high. I am not alone. God is here with me." There is a long, sensitive silence after the note from Bobby is read. You can feel the sadness at his absence and the admiration for his spirit. Bobby is "Cool Hand Luke meets Christ." The gang of ten is like men clinging to each other on a life raft.

Tonight is the last night. The end of the pastoral leadership program at the Q. Each of the men is ready to be certified as a lay minister at the Q or a parish—if they ever get out of prison. Togñi looks around the circle like a Yale dean and asks, "Who should we invite to the graduation ceremony?"

"The bishop," someone says.

"If he can make it," Togñi says, and the bishop will. Bishop Wester is great about coming to the Q. The archbishop as well.

A graduation ceremony is of enormous importance to prisoners because so many have not had much opportunity for learning and because it represents no small sacrifice of time and effort over many, many months. Also, they receive few strokes in their lives for things they can be proud of.

"What about the warden?"

The gang is silent. Then two or three of the group shake their heads. *No.*

"Not after what they did to Bobby."

The bitterness over the perceived injustice to a totally spiritual man is almost palpable. Oscar, an African American lifer in the circle, cocks his head in gentle disagreement. Like Bobby, he himself is "spiritual."

"I think you got Jane [the warden] all wrong. I was in her office when Bobby was sent to the hole and I saw a tear come down her cheek. She felt *bad* about Bobby. *Bad.*"

Oscar knows the warden better than many others. He wins the group over.

So, the bishop comes to the graduation and Warden Jane as well, and all the gang of ten receive their certificates except Bobby. For Bobby "died" when they sent him to the hole. He was transferred from the hole, as often happens, to another prison, Solano, the toughest, cruelest in the state, the inmates tell me. Tougher than Corcoran or Pelican Bay even. He had no chance to exchange hugs or goodbyes with the gang of ten he had come so close to in faith. Men he will likely never see again. He didn't fashion a shiv, or stab anyone in the food-line, or rape a new prisoner, or push drugs. Still he "died." He should have known better. What was he thinking of, advocating for a broader range of ethnic studies at San Quentin College? He had been warned by fellow prisoners to stay away from the brown card activists from Berkeley. After fifteen years he must have just snapped. Or maybe it was a sudden delusion that he could be a person with a voice—if not rights—for a passing moment.

Because once the system's machinery began to churn and grind not even the warden could stop it.

18
JOHN BROWN'S BODY

For almost two years, a man named Joe DeFrancesco has been trying to produce and direct a Broadway play at the Q— Steven Vincent Benét's epic poem *John Brown's Body.* For some time it's been a dream of Joe's, an Academy Award winner out of Lucasfilm in the audiotechnical area. From the beginning he has the support of the warden but getting things done through regular procedures is like kissing a corpse. *Nothing.* Besides, Joe is more of an artist than a politician.

Enter Janet. She was a TA for my college class and is now teaching basic English to the prisoners once a week. Janet is a sixty-year-old mover and shaker. Bright, quick-tongued, stylishly dressed, she soon has the warden and the community resource officer in her purse. One of the reasons is that she is fun and knows how to tweak the system. In no time, she wins the guards over too. She finagles practice times and places, props and financial support, and finally, when Joe is in despair and about to give up—"the show can't go on"—a site for the play, the Protestant chapel. Earl Smith, the Protestant chaplain, had bitterly opposed the use of his chapel as a theater, the same as McManus. "The chapel's a sacred place. Use the cafeteria." But there's no other workable place in the prison and the Protestant chapel has a stage and size that is perfect for the show. So Janet gets to Warden Jane and Jane twists Earl's arm.

As cast members get transferred or put in the hole or released ("tell the warden you want to stay in the Q until the play is over"), Janet is there supporting Joe and keeping the cast nurtured during the long hours of rehearsal. The poor and the outcasts take her back to her days in South America with the Peace Corps, so the mostly Black cast really takes to her. It doesn't hurt that she and her husband Clark love jazz or that she smuggles Kentucky fried chicken, chocolate cake, and other goodies past the guards in her lunch basket. The men haven't gotten this much contraband since Father Jack O'Neill.

One night at a rehearsal in the cramped, oddly shaped room, the power failed and the lights went out. In a prison, it could mean anything. But you have a dozen men with violent pasts alone with an attractive woman. Janet hears men moving in the dark stealthily. She swallows hard, a bit tense. A blonde in the grip of Godzilla? She knows she's a flirt. Silence engulfs the tight, low-roofed room. Then the lights go on. She sees the muscled backs of a dozen men, their hands linked in a protective circle around her.

"Thanks, guys," says Janet, her eyes welling up.

Finally it's Halloween night, 2002. A cast member was released only a short time ago—shaking up the cast so there are last-minute adjustments, and Joe is pulling his hair out. But the performance starts in an hour. I act as one of the "brown cards" accompanying the outside visitors from the East Gate, through the process of having yellow stamped on the back of their hands then to the quad and the chapel. There are 120 people, including the grandson of Steven Vincent Benét, whose short stories I had devoured in my teens. Such a large crowd of visitors is very unusual. For most of them, it is their first time inside a prison. A famous Hollywood director is readying a small chamber-music group whose instruments and voices will provide background and effects. Nearby Lucasfilm has helped support the production. My wife Patty and I sit next to some lifers who greatly appreciate such gestures because it means they're still part of the human race. But most of the visitors, understandably, sit on the left side, the prisoners in blue denim on the right.

As TV and video cameras whir away and the houselights dim, there's excitement in the air. A dozen men in denim take the stage. They are magnificent. With a passion and fervor no one could have imagined, they bring alive Benét's epic poem of slavery and the Civil War. The audience is enthralled and even awed by the men's performance. After the final curtain, the men come off the stage and mingle with the visitors, who are struck, as usual, by the fact that the cast members and other prisoners are human just like themselves. Their perception of men behind bars is changed a bit. Inmates are not all feral beasts. For the men, despite the countless hours of work and sweat, missed phone calls, and lost recreation over the months, the play is something they can be proud of. Prisoners don't perform in Broadway plays. And it's been a chance to transcend the dreariness of their lives—for a short while anyway. When you've been in the Q twenty-five years or so, small pleasures become magnified. It will be all they think about or talk about for days.

Janet is, of course, happy with the play's success and at the same time a little sad. Business is taking her husband out of state. She asks me to visit the cast. I promise. It's a nice entry into a section of the prison that isn't part of my normal run except for the men at the Catholic chapel. "It's a Black prison," Janet assures me confidently. I'm not as sure as she is but in a way she's right. People of color make up 88 percent of the Q and a lot of them are Black. Many of the officers and guards are Black. Maybe she's right, but I won't get to them for a few weeks.

Around Thanksgiving time, I'm roaming the tiers of Donner. Two prisoners tell me they want to become Catholic. One used to be a Mormon.

"There's a lot of good Mormons," I say.

"But I want the original church."

"I'm your man," I say and promise him one of our catechisms. It's the second time we've talked. But he'll probably be moved to God knows where before I can get to him.

The Christmas season has Donner overflowing with a hundred double-stacked beds on the concrete floor. "Broadway"—but not the Broadway brought here two months ago with the play. A hairy, bare-chested guy has a tattoo in the center of his chest. I stop to admire it.

"That looks like the Chrysler 'wings' logo."

"It's the Harley-Davidson," he says, pulling some chest hair away from it.

"Vroom, vroom," I say, twisting an imaginary throttle.

He laughs. He's big enough to be a Hells Angel but a Hells Angel would be put on the high-security Level IV. There's deliberately no apostrophe in Hells Angels, the organization itself says, because there are many different kinds of hell. Any inmate will agree.

I turn toward the cellblocks on the first tier and the guys on psych meds. My last visit is a dark-haired man with an emaciated face. He grips the bars and presses his pale forehead into the black metal that holds him.

"I'll be out in a couple months. I just got cleared for murdering my wife."

"Who killed her?" I'm unprofessionally curious. I read too much crime fiction.

He looks to the left and to the right, then leans confidentially closer to me.

"I did. But you're the first person I ever told."

I am uneasy with his revelation but wonder if he's all there.

"My whole family has this terrible anger. We get violent at times. My parents have a special drug to keep them stable. I wish I could get some of it to replace the drugs and alcohol I use."

We pray.

It's the rainiest December anyone can remember in marvelous Marin County. It will add up to thirty inches with days of blackouts from trees falling on power lines. And at the Q, along with the machine-gun rain and charcoal skies, it's a lockdown Christmas week. It will run almost to New Year's. Depressing. A guard left his jacket lying around for two weeks. An inmate stole the officer's metal star and his cloth badges. So, five-thousand plus men must pay the price. Cell time twenty-four hours a day except for meals. No work, no play, no hanging around. The inmates, who put the worst spin on everything the authorities do—and who are sometimes right—

believe the opportunity for theft was deliberately created by someone. Lockdowns can be easier duty. Plus overtime.

Sadly, because of the lockdown, McManus has to call off the annual Christmas party for the men in the Catholic chapel, their cellies, their friends in the Protestant chapel, and the volunteers and their spouses. It's a beautiful ecumenical moment. All of us of different faiths—Catholics, Protestants, Jews, Muslims, Native Americans—sitting in pews. Downing enchiladas and chocolate cake together, sharing "the bonds of love." The lockdown is a damper on Christmas for me and especially Deacon George who has to get the caterer to swallow the cost for the second year in a row. So on the eve of Christmas, Deacon George and I bring the "Bread of Life," the Eucharist, to the mainliners in North Block and their eyes light up with gratitude.

Before Janet goes out of state, she gives me a short list of Black lifers from *John Brown's Body* to visit. Mid-December I search out the cell of a certain "Large Louie." I spot him naked coming out of the communal shower in North Block, his graying dreadlocks jiggling alongside his head. He is not that tall and I would say he goes at about 350 pounds so he is truly large. But he looks regal as he approaches me and his cell without haste, draping himself in a tired cotton bathrobe. His shape says "sumo wrestler," but when he gives me his steady laser look—not a menacing stare but a size-up—I think Black Mafia.

"Large Louie?" I say.

"That's me." He has a deep, custardy voice.

"Janet sent me."

He smiles benignly. Louie is the lead barber in North Block. He humbly believes he is the most creative "tonsorial artist" around. His own dreadlocks are a masterpiece of intricately braided hair. He shows me the plans he has for a tonsorial parlor and spiritual haven in the community when he gets out. The impressive design includes a play area for little kids. He's been thinking about this. It's easy to be comfortable with this man because he is at peace with himself as he moves thoughtfully, getting ready for his first appointment of the day. It's like he owns the place or like the prison was designed for him: his cell only a few feet away from the sunlit barber shop area on Broadway and the barred communal shower. He's been here longer than most of the guards so he's a force and he is convinced "the reason I'm not outside is God has work for me to do inside." A deep, belly breath. "My role, ya see, is to keep these young Blacks," he points his stubby index finger in a whirly motion at the five-tiered cellblock, "from going back to their violent, sordid pasts."

"You're doing good work here, Louie," I say.

"Give God the glory," he points his finger toward heaven, his words that lovely Black revivalist spirit. "I stonewalled invitations to religious things for years. Then I did *kairos* and my life changed." He pauses, sighs a 350-pound sigh, "and ya know, once you taste the divine you can't walk away." He smiles. "The taste is too sweet."

If there's one thing that impacts the men spiritually at the prison, it's *kairos. Kairos* means the "right moment" for the divine to influence the earthly. Inside the prison, *kairos* is the word inmates use for their own version of Cursillo, an ecumenical lay movement that witnesses to God by extending friendship and concern to others. The word *cursillo* means "little course" of study. Kairos is an intensive three-day experience of God's love for the prisoners and their need to reach out to others with that love. Catholics, Protestants, and Muslins participate, and the impact on the men is remarkable. Large Louie is only one of many.

DOING TIME

A few days later, Deacon George and I find him making Christmas candy for his kids out of Tootsie Rolls. "Happy birthday, Louie," I say.

"God sent you," he says from his cell. "First time I saw you coming down the tier," he jabs his finger at me through the bars, "I knew you were a man of God. You can see it in the face, you can tell." Then he goes on about how great it is that George and I come to visit men in the cells. "I can't tell you what it means to know that someone outside is thinking of us and is willing to come and see us."

"We get more out of it than you do," George and I say almost in unison.

George and I visit a Black man he knows in Badger in South Block. Badger, theoretically, contains heavy-duty prisoners with very long sentences: This man, Teddy, was given ninety-nine years for a crime he never committed. The case is under appeal: "conflicting testimony." Maybe a hapless public defender too. We pray with Teddy, touching fingers through the heavily grated black bars.

Outside in the fresh air, George, a wealth of depressing knowledge (like I will be eventually), scans the yard for officers, then says: "A poor Black in court doesn't have a chance. The public defender he is assigned often lacks the time or motivation, maybe both."

"You know what Johnny Cochran says?" I'm referring to the famous African American lawyer who defended O. J. Simpson.

"No, what?"

"The color of justice is green."

"But sometimes not even that holds true," George says. "I'm close to a wealthy Black couple whose son is at UC Berkeley. He was picked up by the cops *under suspicion*. They said he had to be a drug dealer, otherwise he wouldn't be driving a new Mercedes. His father had to come and bail him out. He's now suing that his son's civil rights were violated."

George gives me his sideways look.

19
INTIMACY

In mid-May, the gang of ten is joined by some laypeople who are interested in prison ministry. Angie, a chemical engineer out of Princeton, currently working on a master's in divinity at GTU in Berkeley, is running a course on the psalms and the Liturgy of the Hours. Togñi and I kibbitz now and then with the men. The laypeople are thrilled, as usual, to be here and to find the inmates not only human but fun.

Angie is in her forties and is worried some convent may reject her because of age. But she brings a degree of computer-aided preparedness—professional, multicolored programs of the Liturgy of the Hours for that day with photographs of various psalm-inspired Holy Land sites—that makes Togñi and me seem like slobs.

Trace, in the expanded circle of chairs, leans forward and in a gravelly voice says how the beginning of Psalm 126 has touched him: *"When Yahweh brought Zion's captives home, at first it seemed like a dream."*

"I found great peace when I accepted the fact that it was God's will I be in jail." He looks down, not around the circle. "But it was hard getting to that point. And it was hard being imprisoned all these years and knowing it was your whole life."

DOING TIME

At this point, a woman in her sixties with frizzled hair and glasses blurts: "I'm not behind bars but I felt imprisoned for thirty-two years."

Everyone in the circle of folding chairs—Angie, Togñi the Jesuit, the inmates, and five laypeople—stare at her, curiously empathetic. She's about to cry, she's so sad.

"Why?" someone asks.

"I was a checker at a supermarket thirty-two years and I hated it."

For a moment, it feels like a T-group, a type of encounter group. We would never have guessed she was a "prisoner" all those years and that her life was like Trace's in some way.

The next Sunday, I preach on intimacy, of all things. Whether from pride, craftsmanship, or spiritual motives, I work hard preparing a homily. I pray, reflect, and struggle all week to come up with a new slant, a new twist that will give the hearers a fresh insight or a new hope or at least keep them awake. And it strikes me that Jesus' words, "Remain in me and I in you," are all about *intimacy*.

"What is intimacy?" I ask the men in orange and a few men in blue. Intimacy means no barriers, I tell them, no defenses, no false fronts. It's total honesty: the sharing of heart and mind and soul and all of one's life. It's hanging in, as the relationship goes through thick and thin, even through sin and failure.

I tell them about a Silicon Valley executive I knew of, who got caught up in the rat race, started drinking heavily, stopped going to Mass, started playing around, and finally had an affair with his wife's best friend. His wife filed for divorce. He said he still loved her but the drinking, the infidelities, and the betrayal of his wife were symptoms of a deeper problem. The intimacy was gone from their marriage. Just as missing Mass, another kind of infidelity, was a symptom of no intimacy with God.

I tell them intimacy is not sex. (At the mention of the word *sex,* one hundred men are fully awake.) Dogs and cats have sex. Intimacy is communion, closeness to the one you love, heart speaking to heart, *I-Thou* as Martin Buber calls it. "Like a face-to-face meeting in the dark," Thomas Merton says, describing prayer—which is nothing if not the desire for intimacy with God. The Gospel of John says, "Remain in me and I in you, for without me you can do nothing."

Unbeknownst to me, Bernie, an apostolic mainliner, has been talking to his cellie about hearing me preach. He is sitting now in the last pew as I speak, on the edge of a sea of orange jumpsuits, his elbows back, his barrel chest out as if sizing me up. After the communion service, Bernie brings him up to meet me.

"I'm Angelo," he says, beaming charisma, shaking my hand enthusiastically, brawly like a boxer.

"He's Puerto Rican," Bernie explains.

"But I'm half-Italian," Angelo says.

"You sound like New York," I say.

"You guessed *right. Hey,* what you said was right on target for me. *Perfect.* Just what I was needing to hear."

"Thanks," I say.

"Youse guys may wonder what impact you have when you talk. Well, it was *big* with me and I want you to know it." He almost thumps my chest with his finger.

I kid him about New York. He tells me about his seventy-year-old mother in Brooklyn saying her beads for him.

He's a regular at the chapel now, at spirituality classes, and at everything, and a lot of fun.

So many prisoners are so muscled like Angelo, so physically developed from manual labor, push-ups, and years on the streets, that I think of them as bodies only. I doubt they can grasp something so ethereal and so beautiful as intimacy with God. And I'm dead wrong—from Trace to Large Louie. In some ways, once they hit bottom, they are more disposed for the spirit than anyone else. They have tried their bodies and found them wanting and have become aware of the spirit within them. I should never doubt that every man has "a spark of the divine," as Dante says, just waiting to be kindled.

A day or so later, I read an article in *Commonweal* by the angry wife of an expriest in Indiana. She was outraged that priest-molesters were receiving salary and benefits upon being defrocked but her pious expriest-husband is getting not a dime and he is struggling. In addition, he is not allowed to be a lector or a Eucharistic minister at the Mass. When I first left the priesthood in the late sixties, it was that way. An expriest was a pariah in the church. But gradually the local practice softened—if you left the diocese where you had been a priest—at least in California. Still, I am reminded that, as an expriest, my involvement in the Eucharist at the Q is highly unusual. Thanks to McManus, I am here.

The next Sunday, after the communion service, two Sisters of Charity, in saris just like Mother Teresa, approach me. They have come to visit the men in the cellblocks.

"What's your name?" one of them asks softly. She is *not* a bubbly nun.

"Dennis Burke." I am decked out in a white alb from head to toe, with a stole around my neck, greeting a horde of departing prisoners.

"Are you a priest?"

"No." Though I don't consecrate the hosts and only distribute the already-consecrated Eucharist, I look, talk, and act like a priest, and every other prisoner is saying "Father," But...

"A deacon?"

"No. I'm an expriest."

"Oh, you're retired and then you came back?" She's not getting it.

"No, I'm married."

"Oh," she says, obviously baffled.

Mother Teresa's nuns strike me as simple and detached. Then again, maybe I'm the one who's not getting it. I've been functioning as a "virtual priest" for a number of years now and have come to believe it's normal. And it's McManus who "called" my reluctant self on board, not me.

The next Monday, I confront McManus in his office. I tell him about the *Commonweal* article and the Sisters of Charity. Then I say:

"Running the communion service and preaching—I just realized *I'm totally illegal*."

McManus breaks into a grin, tosses his hands up, and says:

"That's why we have these big walls here."

We both laugh.

After months of rumors, the time has come: Saturday night, the last day of May, there's a retirement dinner for McManus arranged by the indefatigable Deacon George. Togñi the Jesuit, a Franciscan brother, and fifteen of us long-timers in prison ministry, with our wives sit at a long table at a restaurant in the Berkeley Marina. Through the great bay window we watch the sun set into the water, first pink, then orange, until the distant San Francisco skyline is a silhouette. Most of us have one glass of wine. It's not a drinking crowd. Deacon George has 7-Up. He's been clean and sober for twenty-seven years now. The whole dinner is very simple, the way McManus wants it, "no fuss a'tall." I roast him a little, mimicking his soft Dublin accent: "You have to do something *real-ly, real-ly* bad to get into San Quentin."

Then McManus gets up and says he's done a lot of things in his priestly life—teacher, principal, missionary in Africa, pastor, curate—but his happiest time was his twenty years at San Quentin.

"There's always something different or exciting and it's actually a lot of fun, strangely. And the nice thing about it is you can lock up all your parishioners at 5 p.m. and go home."

The next day is McManus's final Sunday at the Q. The chapel is packed with mainliners in blue and a handful of outside guests. He is an excellent to-the-point preacher and his words are touching.

He says he anguished on Monday, Tuesday, and Wednesday what to say for his final homily at the Q. He prayed about it every day and God answered his prayer on Thursday. He received a note from a prisoner in the hole:

"Dear Father, My granddaughter is being baptized with the name 'Hope' and I don't know any Saint Hope. Could you check and see if there is a saint with that name?"

McManus wrote back:

"I looked everywhere in all the books and couldn't find a Saint Hope. Maybe your granddaughter will be the first one."

Then McManus talked about hope, concluding tenderly: "The one thing I hope is you get out of this awful place."

There is a luncheon afterward for all the prisoners and guests, and as I nibble on fried chicken, chips, and salsa, one of the men in blue sidles up to me and says:

"We're going to miss him but the ones who are going to miss him the most are the men on death row."

20
RACISM

"The Q is a Black prison," my friend Janet said to me before she left. She meant that the Black culture dominates. It's an arguable proposition but close to the truth. San Quentin is 33 percent Black, and 50 percent of all prisoners in America—the most in the world after Russia—are Black. One in three Black men twenty to twenty-nine years of age are in prison or under the criminal justice system. Why? Do they exhibit "clearly defined criminal characteristics," as the Italians, Irish, and Jews were once described as having by the US Immigration Commission in 1911? The true answer is long and multifaceted, but if you want your eyes opened, read *Race to Incarcerate* by Marc Maurer of the Sentencing Project in Washington, DC—a book given to me by a Black prisoner that I stopped to chat with. If I were Black, I think I would tear the buildings down after reading it. Still, some things are obvious even without reading the book: poverty, joblessness, broken school-systems, and single-parent families—because daddy's in jail—are a start.

There's much more, however. It seems that the entire justice system punishes the poor, especially Blacks and Hispanics. Why are the poor jailed in such numbers? They must rely on overworked public defenders who handle as many as fifty cases at the same time. In addition, the laws are often interpreted and enforced differently for whites and Blacks. Whites do drugs in the privacy of their houses. Blacks do it on the street corners of poor neighborhoods heavily patrolled by police. Which group is "picked up" more often? Which gets the more-severe sentence?

Out of state, Janet continues to phone and write cards to the cast of *John Brown*. Father Jack O'Neill, the former chaplain at the Q, does the same with his cons, most of whom are Black. "I spend two hours every morning writing the guys." Encouraged by both of them, I break away from the reception center to get into the suffering Black soul. Something they don't easily let you do. "I'm blessed," they say instinctively, "I'm fine." As they look at you from the cell where they'll probably die.

In February, I drop by to see Bernie in the administration center where he works.

"You have any chance of getting out?"

He shakes his head slowly. "But I got hope. Someday if it's God's will, I'll go free. Right now God must have some special reason for me being here."

I hear that a lot from Black prisoners. *God must have some special reason.*

We talk about parole, and how often prisoners hear the word *no* regardless of how they've changed.

"You sit in your cell for twenty years with nothing to think about except what you did as a twenty-year-old one night on drugs. You change. You grow. Do you really think I'm going to go out and do something to get me back here?"

All the data says the older the prisoner upon release, the less likely he will be rearrested.

Bernie reminds me of the old Duke Ellington number "Mood Indigo," because he doesn't smile easily and he is so soft-spoken his words come forth from some melancholy depth. I can imagine him at some dark blues club in Oakland playing his horn. He was pretty good once.

I find Bernie the next week at the administration center. He's clacking away on his computer board. He nods shyly and we step outside to talk. Then we get to the subject that's making him smoke his cigarette a little too nervously: he's coming up for parole. "I got a spanking clean record," he says as if assuring himself. "I've taken all the courses, finished my college. And I've lined up a temporary job in Visalia as a school janitor—just in case."

"You got a chance, you think?"

"Never know."

But deep in his gut Bernie knows that any man who murdered another—no matter how long ago, no matter how young the man was, no matter how uncharacteristic the act—won't be paroled. Bernie killed a man in a bungled robbery twenty-six years ago but he's not a killer.

Bernie has me thinking. A handgun got him life in prison with little hope of release. If he hadn't carried the gun, hadn't pulled the trigger, he would have been a free man years ago, instead of trapped here with a wasted life. Short on money, high on drugs, he killed a man. But in some ways, Bernie is as much a victim as the man he killed. It's one thing to be poor and Black; it's another to be born that way in America. Burglary rates are the same in Seattle and British Vancouver but burglaries involving a gun (aggravated assault rates) are higher in Seattle. In fact, *eight times higher*. The rate of homicides in Seattle was close to double at the time—388 to 204. Seattle and Vancouver are about a hundred or so miles apart, with the border in between, and yet the demographics of the two cities are almost the same. The moral? You can kill more easily with a gun than anything else. There are handguns in 42 percent of the homes in Seattle but only 12 percent in Vancouver. Canada has very tight laws on handguns. Yet

DOING TIME

America has the highest homicide rate in the world by far and the greatest use of drugs.

The National Rifle Association fights all efforts to control the distribution of handguns, even semiautomatics—the kind used at Columbine by two teenagers. The NRA even held their convention in Columbine—two weeks after the tragedy there. At the same time the NRA also champions maximum sentences and no mercy for men like Bernie. You can't be too tough on crime—but make sure everybody has a gun. It is good for sales.

The state of California is spending $300 million a year to house 8,000 term-to-life inmates *who are eligible for parole.* Yet so few of these inmates move from "eligible" to "released." At some point in the past, a judge said to these inmates, "You will be eligible for parole after seven [or ten or twelve or fifteen years], provided you show good behavior and evidence of rehabilitation." I personally know dozens of lifers like Bernie and Dominic who have done everything they have been asked to do. By any standard I know these men are rehabilitated and ready for release. Why haven't they been?

It reminds me of that wonderful line from comedian Richard Pryor: "Justice? You mean JUST-US." For there's more than a little bit of racism underlying the policy of *tough on crime.* Bernie would agree.

21

SISTER KAREN TEACHES THE PSALMS

Sister Karen is the epitome of the joyful, bouncy, rounded nun in white tennis shoes. She has been playing the guitar and leading the choir at the Sunday communion service and Mass for two years and has fallen in love with the guys. They love her spirit and are aware of her sacrifice—she already teaches five high-school chemistry classes a day, five days a week. Now she has volunteered to teach a course in the parables to the gang of ten. She's not a scripture scholar but she has great notes and enthusiasm from a summer course she took recently. Togñi and I are pleased because we are running out of material. So we kick off the new year—2003.

Karen, though nervous the first night, is meticulously prepared, with freshly typed handouts and questions. She reads from her summer course notes in a slightly grade-school-teacher voice that makes me feel I'm back in fifth grade at first. But the next session she is relaxed, interactive, and perfect.

The prisoners are excited by the parables. As Jeremias, the late, great Protestant scripture scholar, says: The parables were entirely new to their time. "There is nothing like them in rabbinic literature." They reflect with peculiar clarity the character of Jesus' good news and they represent an especially reliable tradition. "We stand right before Jesus when reading his parables." From January on, the guys dig in, tear the parables apart, and make them their own.

DOING TIME

Many Catholics hear a sermon on Sunday but keep the message at arm's length. They go home untouched by the word. Not so with the gang of ten. Everything they hear, everything we discuss about "the word," has personal meaning for them. It turns into a question or a challenge as to how they are living their lives. This is especially true when the subject is forgiveness. I have a harder time forgiving than they do: everyone and thing from the system itself to people who let ambition or indifference cloud their thoughts and emotions when dealing with these guys.

Tonight the parable is about the unforgiving debtor who, after being forgiven the incredible debt of ten thousand talents (millions of dollars) by his master, throttles a fellow servant for not paying him back "five bucks." It's a parable and a subject I've preached on more than once: *unless you forgive from the heart,* as the parable concludes. The gang shares their struggles with bitterness and anger, and with forgiving certain people in the past. Triggered by their scathingly honest revelations of their failures and successes in forgiving, I examine my own conscience. I confess to them that I have forgiven all my enemies, all those who have done me wrong—and from the heart *I thought*—but some keep coming back and I have to forgive them again.

The group smiles slyly at my words for they have to keep forgiving again and again too, but I am amazed by their equanimity day after dreary day. Humans are remarkably resilient, able to resign themselves to such a terrible life as at the Q— with God's grace. But later, I'm talking to Trace as he fingers the purple diamond tattooed on the back of his hand.

"I've forgiven everyone or I try. You can't hang on to things from the past. You got to move on." He pauses and looks like he's going to cry almost, but Trace never cries. He breathes in and out deliberately, as if he is about to say something he can't quite understand. "I can never pay back the life that I took. But I have more than paid back the sentence I was given by the judge: twenty years, plus five. I keep waiting." He chokes ever so slightly. "I wonder where the mercy is."

I do too.

Sometimes I realize my experience with the gang of ten makes me imagine I'm in a monastery of good spiritual men. There are plenty of bad dudes here who do drugs and pruno, who seethe quietly with bitterness, and who are ever on the edge of violence. So when Tito, my cheery Filipino friend, stops me for a chat, I ask him how much genuine spirituality there really is in the prison. He's been around and he's seen it all.

"Probably 10 percent of the mainliners are 'spiritual.' They're moving toward God or they've had some kind of conversion. That's about right, I think." He pushes his hands in the pockets of his denim jacket. It's January and still a bit brisk. He thinks about what he's said. "I forgave everybody long ago." There's that *forgive* word again. "You have to be open. Everybody sees everything in prison. They wave to you as you sit on your toilet in your cell." He laughs. "And they see you naked in the shower. We're all naked together." He laughs again. "You have to forgive. You can't go around blaming everybody. And this prison, San Quentin, is the best for that. I mean—for finding God. There's all kinds of opportunity: classes, prayer groups, chapel, Bible studies, our group [gang of ten]. There's so much support and community for God in your life. There's no place like the Q."

That's my impression as well and Warden Jane has something to do with that—all the outside community resources. But I worry because a great deal more could be done if prisons could move from punishment to rehabilitation.

DOING TIME

"Why are we educating this trash? Spend your energy with people on the outside," a guard says to one of the teachers. Guards are guards and have been trained only in the area of punishment. The other side needs to be there too.

Deacon George tells me that one day he was walking toward West Block with a guard. The guard says: "You know the only difference between *those* guys behind bars and us? They're after fast money. We take ours slow."

A day or two later, I get a call from a woman in San Mateo who runs a soup kitchen and who wants to check on a recent arrival in the reception center. I find Salvatore on "Broadway," outside the cells on the first tier of Donner. He's leaning on one of the double-stacked beds, eyeing the traffic: guys moving and dealing cigarettes, coffee, ramen noodles, whatever. One of the guards is taking count, prisoners are out on the floor getting haircuts. They're back from breakfast and it's busy, busy, like the opening scene from *Guys and Dolls*.

Within breathless seconds, Salvatore is telling me he has been in and out of prison and rehab for years and even graduated from Delancey Street, the French Foreign Legion of rehab.

"Guys leave Delancey Street, and the first night out they buy a hooker, get some stash or coke, and are higher than the national debt. We're all liars and con men."

Salvatore is a hyper, curly haired, fast-talking racetrack kind of guy. He's topless, exposing his very hairy chest, distended belly, and a host of tattoos. For prisoners, tattoos are a way of saying: "I'm into *the life*." I note one of a pretty girl on one shoulder and a girl's name, Lynette, on the other.

"Don't ever tattoo a girl's name on your body. How do you explain it to the next girl." He shows me a small tattoo intricately designed with his name and another girl's, almost buried in deep chest hair.

"Why did you break up? Those tattoos are pretty permanent."

"I'm Maltese, she's Italian, so it was *boom* all the time." He smashes his fists together. Laughs.

He talks about his work of repairing and selling cars on the outside. He talks about knowing the good Catholic lady who sent me to him. She's been helping him for years. Then he says, a bit shamefacedly:

"I'm Catholic but I go to some Christian Church. I really can't get *the word* at the Catholic Church."

I can't disagree. My Maltese friend may be looking for a quick fix but the Pentecostals make the *word* simple, central, emotional—appealing to the poor much better than many priests do. The Pentecostals get them fired up. The Catholic Mass, on the other hand, assumes a sense of the holy and a fairly high degree of understanding and faith in the Eucharist: the worship of God over the good-feelings experience. The problem with the stress on faith as feelings and experience, however, is that it tends to exclude the use of the mind. In Catholic faith, there are no quick fixes. Faith is the gift of God but on man's side it feels like a hard-bought thing.

Most "Christians" at the Q are not fanatics. They are simple Mexicans or poor whites struggling with addiction or violence. Outside the Q they are too-often Christians in name only or maybe in desire or maybe in their struggle to overcome their destructive tendencies—just like the Catholics. They're all like some poor guy clinging to a twig on the side of a cliff. So, why am I so bugged by Fundamentalism and their extremists? Why? I see myself as a Christian humanist who believes in the axiom of Thomas Aquinas: grace builds on nature. *Gratia supponit naturam.* And when human nature is deformed in some way, not fully or authentically involved in the process of grace, then grace, God, and Jesus can "come out" twisted. The extremist view of life is fear-based and shuts down the mind. One can't really think about it. And a heart without a mind is dangerous. Faith becomes a one-dimensional caricature: me and Jesus.

22
DEATH ROW

April light streams through the chapel windows and hovers over Russ's head. I watch him fondly, having instructed him the past six months. He is still, quiet, absorbed by the event that has taken place. This funny, loquacious man, full of gestures, now radiates the secret joy of his baptism, Holy Saturday Night 2004.

A crystal spring morning I am walking down to the lower yard and I see some recently deposited prisoners behind the "reception fence." I approach and a fine-looking Black man comes up close to the fence.

He looks desperate, as if he might cry. He tells me about his baby boy in the hospital, the left side of his face all swollen up with a spider bite.

"You here on parole violation?"

"No. I've been off drugs three years. I was nine days away from being off parole. *Nine days.* And they drag me in."

"What happened?" There's a wholesomeness about him.

"Some guy cut my throat with a knife," he stretches his neck to show me a very thin scar on his throat that is easy to miss, "and I get thrown back in."

"What did you do?"

"Nothin.' I wasn't guilty of anything. But I was told if I was some place where I got cut, then I was probably some place I shouldn't have been. *Nine days*. I'll probably lose my job now and my family. *Nine days*."

We link our fingers through the storm fence. Tears are rolling down his cheeks. He's a big strong man. I promise to pray for him and his child. He's enormously grateful. But I am angry. A system that so easily tears him away from his job. And no concern for the mother or child. *Nine days*. No judge, no jury, no parole.

I walk the upper yard, the length of the corrugated metal roof, and approach the locked gate. A light-haired guard asks who I'm looking for.

"Ronnie Bell."

He opens the gate. I follow him into the East Block where two guards are talking. They stop and give me attention, trying to be helpful. I'm a little nervous. I expect to be met with hard questions. Technically, I'm not supposed to be here. There was no "Death Row" sign painted calligraphically on the wall as there is on the other end of East Block. But I sense I'm here now—Death Row.

"2 East 80," I say, reading the note Jack O'Neill had given me.

"Right up there," one of the guards points the direction. I trudge up the metal stairs to the second tier. 280 East. Ron is not there.

"He's been transferred," the sleepy occupant of the cell informs me. I go back and tell the guards and they show some concern. They check their logs.

"He stays in his cell usually," the guard answers me with a kind of nurturing knowledge. I get the sense they know these men pretty well and have gotten close to them after all the years. "You might check outside. He may have come out today."

Immediately outside, in a tight quarter court, a fierce basketball game is going on. Big muscular Black men climbing the sky for a rebound. I look over the bodies grunting and groaning. For some reason I thought "death row" meant you never left your cell. I check with a few inmates standing around watching. They're very friendly. Ron Bell isn't here.

I go inside and tell the guard and he begins to show some administrative concern like, "Where could he be? He should be in his cell by *my* log." He checks my note from Jack O'Neill.

"Oh, it's *fourth tier.*"

He grins. This place is like a neighborhood.

All this time, I have felt some serious concern. I'm breaking the rules, I shouldn't be here, and this cellblock has six-hundred killers who have nothing to lose. But I'm getting used to the place now. Outside of Richard Allen Davis and a half-dozen serial killers, it's just like the rest of the Q.

I bang up the steel staircase to the fourth tier. At the top I run into the most beautiful woman guard at San Quentin. Tall, Hispanic, movie-star face, eyes of a toreador. She looks me over sourly and opens the tier gate with a big rattle of keys. I walk down the tier to 4 East 80.

"Ron Bell?"

"That's me."

"Jack O'Neill sent me, said to be sure and look up Ron Bell."

"Jack O'Neill? I just love the man. He's sending me cards all the time. Here's one." He quickly sorts through papers, books, letters, cards, a headset, a half-buried TV cluttered and clumped on a bed he obviously doesn't sleep on. His cell is a tight little closet. He drags out a card. "Lookee here."

The card is a comic picture of a Black babe in white ermine with O'Neill's handwriting: "This lady was asking for you." We laugh. "He's always sending me cards."

Ron is a sweet, cackle-laughing Black man of forty-two but looks and sounds much older. His teeth are bad and—unlike most Black inmates—his head is unshaven. He has a graying hairline combed back and rising.

He starts talking about Santa Rosa.

"I loved it there in Santa Rosa. Worked at the country club, sweepin' and things. The people were wonderful to me."

Forgetting I'm on Death Row, I ask: "Is there a chance of getting out?"

"Oh yeah," he says with unbridled enthusiasm, "I didn't do the crime. A woman witness lied about me. We have her written testimony to that effect. We just need a graphologist to verify it's her handwriting."

Deacon George tells me six out of six-hundred men on Death Row own up to doing it. God knows. But Ronnie keeps going on as cheerful as a gospel singer mentioning "the Lord" again and again. And I wonder how a man can keep his spirits up locked in a cage for twenty years. A sweep-up man in a country club. Then he looks up, smiling, and assures me "If my appeal doesn't go through—the Lord will take me home."

23

THINGS I HAVE LEARNED

The soap-opera noir that is the Q continues through the warm summer months into the cool autumn nights. The unpredictable is predictable as ever: an inmate falls five tiers to the concrete below and shatters his legs. No one knows how or why.

In the yard, a gentle, rounded man with a frizzy, gray beard and a turban stops me.

"I am Sikh," he says with a heavy accent. "Can you get me book for prayers?"

"I don't have one handy on the shelf but I will see what I can do." Later, the poor Sikh is written up for not shaving off his beard, although shaving it off is against his religion.

And so it goes, on and on from tragedy to comedy, from tears to laughter. But my time at the Q has finally come to an end.

So, what have I learned from almost ten years at the Q? Above everything else, a love for the prisoners. From the very first, there was a certain edge in entering a prison and mingling with killers, rapists, drug dealers, and extortionists. But when I got to know them, listening to their sad stories, they became ordinary people to me. They welcomed me when I came and thanked me when I left. With nothing but time on their hands and no place to go, there was always a certain lazy tranquility about them, a softness amidst their evident muscularity—especially the gang of ten.

I learned a killer is not a killer unless he wants to kill again. I never encountered a prisoner who wanted to kill again.

It was the most horrific moment of his life. Hardened types soften with age. They drop from the gangs that got them into trouble in the first place. They get a job in the prison, go to school, sometimes to church, read the Bible perhaps. They soften and change and wait. Eight-thousand men have perfect records in prison but no parole. And yet, the recidivism rate for homicides is lower than for any other crime—1 percent.

A killing is a terrible thing, but a fit of a young man's temper or a drug habit explains many a murder. I would like to see a man after fifteen or twenty years in prison be given a fair hearing as to what he's like now—not how he was twenty or thirty years ago.

There was a fairly high degree of spirituality evident among some. They seemed to pray all the time. They knew they were in for a long time so they adjusted to the fact: "I guess the Lord wants me here a while longer"—after being turned down for parole for the umpteenth time. Their acceptance of their punishment with patient resignation, year after year, is impressive.

The rich tend to be more distant than the poor. I noticed it in my first assignment as a parish priest. The people in the suburbs were nice enough but cool, as their heady children would size me up in the schoolyard. When I took a group of the boys up to the seminary during vocation week, one parent commented: "You're trying to make them all priests?" The next parish was lower middle class, and the kids grabbed me by the cassock and shouted, "Hi, Father" *every* time they saw me. There were no barriers, no defenses. They were hot, not cool. The prisoners are mostly the poor so they are warmer generally, especially with people they know and trust. They are like children in that sense. I suppose I'm trying to say the sheer humanity of the men at the

DOING TIME

Q was the humanity of the poor—warm and embracing and in need of anything you can do.

I never felt closer to Christ than when I was carrying the Eucharist in the pyx in my pocket across the yard, past the adjustment center and the library, to the men in the cellblocks. Christ was in the Eucharist and he was in the men in the cellblocks as well. "I was in prison and you visited me" was ever on my mind and in my motivation. You might say I'm idealizing this awful place. But ask anyone who has become involved—McManus, O'Neill, Deacon George—and they will tell you it gets in your blood and won't let you go. And the men themselves are the reward.

What else have I learned? The vast overwhelming need for change in the prison and justice system. Mandatory sentencing, the "3-strikes" policy, the delay or refusal of parole—these things must change. The long, unending sentences must come to an end. The death penalty must give way to life. Time must be more than time. It's the time of their lives.

—⚥—

So, the time has come. I'm going to miss those cool, damp mornings, walking with the great San Francisco Bay on my left, into King's Castle with its crenellated towers. Waving to lifers around the chapel door or pruning the rose bushes. Bantering with McManus, Deacon George, and the new chaplain, Father Stephen, before attacking the cellblocks and five-thousand stories. Preaching to the bent, pained, misshapen men from Alpine, Donner, and points west.

Over the years, men have assured me that I did more for them, sharing their isolation from the world, than they did for me. But the opposite is true. I got more out of being with the men at the Q than they could imagine. Their refreshingly honest humanity. No facades, no games, and infectious humor and amazing patience with their lot. Never would you find so many young, able-bodied men standing around with nothing to do but time. So, this awful place has been beautiful for me and a source of amazing grace. I won't forget its funny old buildings, the men in blue and in orange, and my time with them at the Q. It was a gift.

24
I WAS IN PRISON AND YOU VISITED ME

The Catholic Church was founded by a "death row inmate" and some excons: Jesus, Peter, and Paul. They all "did time." Paul was a repeat offender: *"I have been sent to prison more often, and whipped so many times more, often almost to death."* He was under house arrest for two years in Rome. Peter was miraculously released from prison, but he, along with Paul, eventually joined Jesus in suffering the death penalty.

How did Jesus feel after he had been arrested? Much like the men at the Q: abandoned; deserted by his loyal followers, the apostles; betrayed by one of them; rejected by the world that had hung on his every word and was now crying for his blood; being mocked, scourged, ridiculed. He must have felt it was the low point of his human life: sitting in a dirty cell, bloody and beaten, waiting for the executioners, praying to the Father for them, for *"they know not what they do."* So Jesus knows what it is like to be caged in a cell. Jesus can identify with prisoners. He was one himself. Christ felt abandoned even by his Father. He cried out: *"My God, my God, why have you abandoned me?"*

How could this be? Christ—who is existence itself, the source of our being, our every movement, our very breath, the thump of our hearts, without whom we would cease to be and never would have been, the Lord of the stars, the universe, the Lord of light and unspeakable power—feeling ridiculed, betrayed, rejected, and even abandoned by his Father? In the first century, the early heresies denied the humanity of Christ. Jesus only *appeared* to be human, but it was just a disguise. They were the Docetists, from the Latin word *docet,* which means "it appears or seems." The Gnostics, from the Greek word for *knowledge,* believed they had a secret knowledge of God. They saw the flesh, sex, and marriage as evil and unspiritual, and they denied that the Son of God could ever have taken on evil flesh. Later, Eutyches would teach Monophysitism: one nature only in Christ—the divine. Jesus' humanity was like a drop of water in the ocean of his divinity. Eutyches could not believe God would stoop to becoming a man. Since that time, we have tended to stress his divinity so much, especially in unbelieving times, that he easily becomes like a holy card Jesus, riding the clouds high up there, disengaged and uninvolved with "our stuff" down here. But Christ is right here with us. He has been through rejection, betrayal, and abandonment and he stays with us through ours.

Prisoners have spoken often to me about feeling abandoned. They worry the world has forgotten them and in fact it has very often. They are used to the awful food (the state pays $2.75 per man per day, so supplementing the food is hard), the rules, the confinement, the nastiness of some guards and some other prisoners, and so on. But this sense of abandonment becomes a terrible loneliness. Their sons and daughters are growing up without them. A letter arrives from a wife explaining that after waiting ten years she has decided to file for divorce. People are born and die without their presence. If prisoners do get out, there's not much of a future left and what there is of it looks pretty bleak.

In one of the most beautiful and leveling passages in the New Testament, Jesus speaks of the Last Judgment (Matthew 25:31–46). "Come, you that are blessed by my Father....For I was hungry and you gave me food; I was thirsty and you gave me drink; I was a stranger and you welcomed me; naked and you gave me clothing; I was sick and you took care of me; I was in prison and you visited me. Then the righteous will answer him, 'Lord,...when was it that we saw you in prison and visited you?' And the response: "In so far as you did this to the least of my brothers, you did it to me."

Jesus ranks visiting anyone in prison the same as visiting him. It's right up there with feeding the hungry. Why did Jesus "throw in" visiting him in prison? Didn't he know that prisoners are despicable and outside the bounds of society? Most people shudder at the thought of them. "They should lock them up and throw away the key. They are all a bunch of no goods."

Why did Jesus identify so intimately with who today would be druggies, burglars, and killers? Well, we know he was a prisoner himself. But more than that, Jesus loved the poor, the outcasts, the pariahs. And who represents them better than a prisoner locked in a cell and abandoned? They come from impoverished neighborhoods, broken-down schools, and homes that were not homes at all. The majority of them cannot read or write and they lack a skill or a trade. Our prison systems hold them in contempt, for the most part, punishing them rather than rehabilitating them. They are the "Cool Hand Lukes," the poorest of the poor. Jesus identified with the poor more than any other group. "Blessed are the poor," he said, and "Woe to you rich." He didn't mean you are good because you are poor but that you are more open to the gospel message than the rich.

The Pharisees were scandalized by Jesus. *"He welcomes sinners and eats with them."* They believed God's mercy was limited to people like them, upright and respectable. Their vision did not include sinners: the lame, crippled, tax collectors and, of course, cons and excons. Jesus shows that God's mercy breaks through all the limits we try to put on it. He tells us that God is as foolish with his mercy as a father who welcomes back with open arms a son who has become a pork-eating Gentile.

One Sunday, I was at San Quentin reading the gospel of the prodigal son. The father looks out every day into the distance for his lost son. The older son keeps telling him what a bum the younger son is but the father doesn't hear him. He doesn't care that the younger son stiffed him. He's already forgiven him because this father is a fool for love.

At the part that said the son had reached the dregs, I stopped. Looking out at 150 prisoners in orange jumpsuits with sad, bleary, defeated faces, tattoos on their eyelids and arms, some with walrus mustaches, I asked: "How many here have reached the dregs?" To a man, they raised their hands. It was a moment of pure honesty: "I've sinned." It was a beautiful moment to me because, for some, it meant the first step of the long road home.

But back to the younger son, mumbling about his unworthiness to be a son. The father doesn't hear. He is so filled with joy that his son is no longer lost, he has already forgiven him. He is shouting orders: Get him some fresh clothes and sandals and a ring for his finger, and let's celebrate with the fatted calf because my son has come back to life.

How do we explain such a father? A father so prodigal with his mercy? I tell the men at the Q, if God the father were singing a country-western song, it would go: "You keep letting me down and I keep picking you up 'cuz I'm just a fool for love."

The prodigal son meets the prodigal father. To me that's the story of prison: the possibility of repentance, the possibility of conversion. Prisoners have lonely hours, weeks, months, years to mull over their crime. It plays over and over in their nightmare dreams. Most offenses were done in their wild teens and twenties. I have seen men mellow and bloom with faith and repentance over some sordid past they couldn't forget. But they need help along the way.

Perhaps the idea of reaching out to prisoners struck you as you read through these pages. Go for it. For God shows his touching mercy now through you and me. We are the hands and feet of Christ, his eyes and ears. A few minutes listening to their stories, a word of kindness through the cell bars, may be the start of something beautiful for God. And beautiful for you, as you hear the words of Christ echoing in your ear: *"I was in prison and you visited me."*